IMMIGRATION IN THE 21ST CENTURY: POLITICAL, SOCIAL AND ECONOMIC ISSUES

PRESIDENTIAL EXECUTIVE ACTION ON IMMIGRATION

OVERVIEW AND ISSUES

IMMIGRATION IN THE 21ST CENTURY: POLITICAL, SOCIAL AND ECONOMIC ISSUES

Additional books in this series can be found on Nova's website under the Series tab.

Additional e-books in this series can be found on Nova's website under the e-book tab.

IMMIGRATION IN THE 21ST CENTURY: POLITICAL, SOCIAL AND ECONOMIC ISSUES

PRESIDENTIAL EXECUTIVE ACTION ON IMMIGRATION

OVERVIEW AND ISSUES

DAVID FERGUSON
EDITOR

nova publishers
New York

Library of Congress Cataloging-in-Publication Data

ISBN: 978-1-63482-263-3

Published by Nova Science Publishers, Inc. † New York

CONTENTS

Preface		**vii**
Chapter 1	Executive Discretion as to Immigration: Legal Overview *Kate M. Manuel and Michael John Garcia*	**1**
Chapter 2	The Obama Administration's November 2014 Immigration Initiatives: Questions and Answers *Kate M. Manuel*	**39**
Chapter 3	The President's Immigration Accountability Executive Action of November 20, 2014: Overview and Issues *William A. Kandel, Jerome P. Bjelopera, Andorra Bruno and Alison Siskin*	**73**
Index		**119**

PREFACE

This book provides an overview of the executive action on immigration, and well as discusses the issues involved.

Chapter 1 – President Obama announced in June 2014 that he would seek "to fix as much of our immigration system as I can on my own" through administrative action. It seems likely that such actions will prompt heated legal debate concerning the scope of the Executive's discretionary authority over immigration matters, including with respect to the enforcement of immigration-related sanctions and the granting of immigration benefits or privileges. Such debate may be similar to that which followed the 2012 launch of the executive initiative commonly known as Deferred Action for Childhood Arrivals (DACA), under which certain unlawfully present aliens who were brought to the United States as children may be granted "deferred action" (a type of relief from removal) and work authorization. While some have argued that DACA constitutes an abdication of the Executive's duty to enforce the laws and runs afoul of specific requirements found in the Immigration and Nationality Act (INA), others have argued that the initiative is a lawful exercise of the discretionary authority conferred on the Executive by the Constitution and federal statute. Executive discretion over immigration matters is informed (and, in some instances, circumscribed) by statutory delegations of authority and constitutional considerations. In some cases, a particular immigration policy or initiative might be premised on multiple sources of discretionary authority. These sources include the following: *Express delegations of discretionary authority by statute.* In some instances, the INA grants the Executive broad discretion to provide certain forms of relief or benefits (e.g., work authorization or temporary protected status) to foreign nationals. In other instances, the INA permits immigration authorities to waive the application of requirements which would otherwise render an alien ineligible for particular immigration benefits. The INA also gives the Executive broad "parole" authority, under which immigration officials may sometimes permit aliens to physically enter or remain in the country without such entry or presence constituting "admission" for immigration purposes. Any exercises of such statutory authority must be consistent with the terms of the delegation (although the executive branch might have some discretion in interpreting the statute, as discussed below). *Prosecutorial or enforcement discretion deriving from the Executive's independent constitutional authority.* The Executive is generally recognized as possessing some degree of independent authority in assessing whether to prosecute apparent violations of federal law. However, specific statutory mandates could be seen as limiting the Executive's discretion to take particular actions (e.g., by requiring that certain aliens be detained pending removal proceedings). The express adoption of a policy that constitutes an abdication of a statutory duty could also be found to be impermissible, but it might be difficult for a court to assess the degree of nonenforcement that would entail an "abdication." *Discretion in interpreting and applying immigration law.* The Supreme Court has found that some deference may be owed to agency regulations (or adjudications) which construe statutes that are "silent or ambiguous" as to specific issues. The executive branch may also be afforded deference in less formal interpretations of statutes and in interpreting its own regulations. However, agency interpretations must conform to the "unambiguously expressed intent of Congress."

Chapter 2 – On November 20, 2014, President Obama delivered a televised address wherein he broadly described the steps that his administration is taking to "fix" what he has repeatedly described as a "broken immigration system." Following the President's address, executive agencies made available intra-agency memoranda and fact sheets detailing specific actions that have already been taken, or will be taken in the future. These actions generally involve either border security, the current unlawfully present population, or future legal immigration. The most notable of these actions, for many commentators, are the initiatives to grant "deferred action"—one type of relief from removal—to some unlawfully present aliens who were brought to the United States as children and raised here, or who have children who are U.S. citizens or lawfully permanent resident (LPR) aliens. Previously, in June 2012, then Secretary of Homeland Security Janet Napolitano announced a program—commonly known as Deferred Action for Childhood Arrivals (DACA)—whereby unlawfully present aliens who had been brought to the United States as children and met other criteria could receive deferred action and, in many cases, employment authorization. The eligibility criteria for DACA expressly excluded unlawfully present aliens who were over 31 years of age, or who had entered the United States on or after June 15, 2007. However, aliens who are over 31 years of age, or entered between June 15, 2007, and January 1, 2010, could receive deferred action as part of the 2014 initiative. Similarly, unlawfully present aliens who have children who are U.S. citizens or LPRs could also receive deferred action and employment authorization pursuant to the November 2014 initiatives, provided they meet specified criteria. These criteria include "continuous residence" in the United States since before January 1, 2010; physical presence in the United States both on the date the initiative was announced and on the date when they request deferred action; and not being an enforcement priority (e.g., not a threat to national or border security). The announced executive actions—particularly the granting of deferred action and employment authorization to unlawfully present aliens—have revived debate about the President's discretionary authority over immigration like that which followed the announcement of DACA in 2012. In the case of DACA, some argued that the initiative violates the Take Care Clause of the U.S. Constitution, runs afoul of specific requirements found in the Immigration and Nationality Act (INA), or is inconsistent with historical precedents. Others, however, asserted that DACA involves a valid exercise of the executive's prosecutorial or enforcement discretion, is consistent with the INA, and has ample historical precedent. Similar arguments will likely be made as to the November 2014 actions, which affect a significantly larger number of aliens than DACA. Legal challenges to DACA have generally failed on standing grounds, because the plaintiffs bringing these challenges were not seen as the proper parties to seek judicial relief from a federal court. The one exception to this—the litigation in *Crane v. Napolitano*—resulted in the reviewing federal district court finding that DACA runs afoul of provisions in Section 235 of the INA which some assert require the executive to place unlawfully present aliens in removal proceedings. However, this same federal district court subsequently found that it lacked jurisdiction because the plaintiff immigration officers alleged that they faced discipline by their employer, DHS, if they refused to implement DACA, and such claims are within the jurisdiction of the Merit Systems Protection Board (MSPB), not the court. The 113th Congress has also considered legislation to defund DACA (e.g., H.R. 5272, H.R. 5316).

Chapter 3 – On November 20, 2014, President Obama announced his Immigration Accountability Executive Action which revises some U.S. immigration policies and initiates several programs, including a revised border security policy for the Southwest border; deferred action programs for some unauthorized aliens; revised interior enforcement priorities; changes to aid the entry of skilled workers; the promotion of immigrant integration and naturalization; and several other initiatives the President indicated would improve the U.S. immigration system. The most controversial among these provisions will grant deferred action to as many as 5 million unauthorized aliens.

In: Presidential Executive Action on Immigration ISBN: 978-1-63482-263-3
Editor: David Ferguson

Chapter 1

EXECUTIVE DISCRETION AS TO IMMIGRATION: LEGAL OVERVIEW*

Kate M. Manuel and Michael John Garcia

SUMMARY

President Obama announced in June 2014 that he would seek "to fix as much of our immigration system as I can on my own" through administrative action. It seems likely that such actions will prompt heated legal debate concerning the scope of the Executive's discretionary authority over immigration matters, including with respect to the enforcement of immigration-related sanctions and the granting of immigration benefits or privileges. Such debate may be similar to that which followed the 2012 launch of the executive initiative commonly known as Deferred Action for Childhood Arrivals (DACA), under which certain unlawfully present aliens who were brought to the United States as children may be granted "deferred action" (a type of relief from removal) and work authorization. While some have argued that DACA constitutes an abdication of the Executive's duty to enforce the laws and runs afoul of specific requirements found in the Immigration and Nationality Act (INA), others have argued that the initiative is a lawful exercise of the discretionary authority conferred on the Executive by the Constitution and federal statute.

---

* This is an edited, reformatted and augmented version of a Congressional Research Service publication, No. R43782, dated November 10, 2014.

Executive discretion over immigration matters is informed (and, in some instances, circumscribed) by statutory delegations of authority and constitutional considerations. In some cases, a particular immigration policy or initiative might be premised on multiple sources of discretionary authority. These sources include the following:

- ***Express delegations of discretionary authority by statute.*** In some instances, the INA grants the Executive broad discretion to provide certain forms of relief or benefits (e.g., work authorization or temporary protected status) to foreign nationals. In other instances, the INA permits immigration authorities to waive the application of requirements which would otherwise render an alien ineligible for particular immigration benefits. The INA also gives the Executive broad "parole" authority, under which immigration officials may sometimes permit aliens to physically enter or remain in the country without such entry or presence constituting "admission" for immigration purposes. Any exercises of such statutory authority must be consistent with the terms of the delegation (although the executive branch might have some discretion in interpreting the statute, as discussed below).
- ***Prosecutorial or enforcement discretion deriving from the Executive's independent constitutional authority.*** The Executive is generally recognized as possessing some degree of independent authority in assessing whether to prosecute apparent violations of federal law. However, specific statutory mandates could be seen as limiting the Executive's discretion to take particular actions (e.g., by requiring that certain aliens be detained pending removal proceedings). The express adoption of a policy that constitutes an abdication of a statutory duty could also be found to be impermissible, but it might be difficult for a court to assess the degree of nonenforcement that would entail an "abdication."
- ***Discretion in interpreting and applying immigration law.*** The Supreme Court has found that some deference may be owed to agency regulations (or adjudications) which construe statutes that are "silent or ambiguous" as to specific issues. The executive branch may also be afforded deference in less formal interpretations of statutes and in interpreting its own regulations. However, agency interpretations must conform to the "unambiguously expressed intent of Congress."

In June 2014, President Barack Obama announced that he would seek "to fix as much of our immigration system as I can on my own" through administrative action.[1] The President reiterated his intent to act before the end of the year in a November 5, 2014, press conference.[2] Commentators have suggested that the executive actions could affect significantly more unlawfully present aliens than the earlier Deferred Action for Childhood Arrivals (DACA) initiative.[3] This initiative, which began in 2012, has permitted over 500,000 aliens to obtain "deferred action" (one type of relief from removal) and, in many cases, work authorization.[4]

DACA has prompted heated legal debate about the permissibility of the executive branch's actions. Some have argued that the DACA initiative is a lawful exercise of the discretionary authority conferred on the Executive by the Constitution and federal statute.[5] However, others have argued that the initiative impinges on congressional authority to regulate immigration, constitutes an abdication of the Executive's duty to enforce the laws, or runs afoul of specific provisions of the Immigration and Nationality Act (INA).[6] It seems likely that whatever actions the Obama Administration may announce in late 2014 will prompt similar debate, particularly as to the scope of the Executive's discretionary authority over immigration matters.

This debate ultimately reflects the respective roles that Congress and the executive branch play in the nation's constitutional system of government. Article I of the Constitution expressly grants the power to legislate to Congress, and Congress has exercised this power as to immigration, in part, by enacting the INA.[7] The INA provides a comprehensive set of rules governing the admission of foreign nationals into the United States and the conditions of such aliens' continued presence in the country, including their eligibility to obtain employment or public benefits, adjust immigration status, and become U.S. citizens. In addition, the INA establishes various mechanisms for enforcing these rules, including by prescribing the removal of aliens found to have entered the United States without permission, or to have violated the terms governing their authorized admission into the country.[8] It also established criminal penalties for certain immigration violations.[9]

On the other hand, the INA expressly or impliedly confers some discretionary authority on the executive branch in matters of immigration enforcement.[10] For example, the INA authorizes immigration officials to grant certain types of benefits or relief to qualifying aliens who lack lawful immigration status. Moreover, the INA permits immigration officials to waive certain statutory restrictions that might otherwise render an alien ineligible to receive particular immigration benefits.[11] The exercise of these discretionary authorities may enable some unlawfully present aliens to remain in the United States—through asylum,[12] temporary protected status,[13] cancellation of removal,[14] or some other means—rather than being removed.

In other cases, however, aliens who have entered or have stayed in the United States in violation of INA requirements may be permitted to remain in the country and, in some cases, legalize their status, not as the result of the exercise of expressly delegated authority, but as a result of the executive branch's independent discretion in enforcing the law.[15]Article II of the Constitution specifically tasks the Executive to "take Care that the Laws be faithfully executed," and the executive branch has historically been seen as having some discretion (commonly known as prosecutorial or enforcement discretion) in determining when, against whom, how, and even whether to prosecute apparent violations of the law. For example, immigration officials may opt to give a lower priority to the removal of certain categories of unlawfully present aliens because the removal of other categories (e.g., those convicted of serious crimes) has been deemed a higher priority in light of resource constraints and other considerations.[16] Congressional enactments could, however, be seen as limiting the executive's discretion not to take particular actions (e.g., by mandating that certain aliens be detained pending removal proceedings).[17] The express adoption of an executive policy that is "in effect an abdication of ... statutory duty" could also be found to be impermissible,[18] but it might be difficult for a court to assess the degree of nonenforcement that would entail an "abdication."

The executive branch's discretion to interpret applicable statutes when Congress has not spoken to the precise question at issue may also afford immigration officials some flexibility in determining how INA requirements apply to a particular alien or category of aliens.[19] This discretion may be relevant in determining how particular statutory grants of discretionary authority are to be applied (e.g., what constitutes "exceptional and extremely unusual hardship" for purposes of cancellation of removal, or "extreme hardship" for purposes of certain waivers of inadmissibility).[20] It can also play a role in determining whether and how particular statutes are seen to circumscribe the Executive's enforcement discretion. That is, where a statute is silent or ambiguous as to the circumstances of its enforcement in particular cases, the Executive may have some discretion in determining its application.[21]

This report provides an overview of the three broad types of discretion that the Executive can be seen to have as to immigration: (1) express delegations of discretionary authority; (2) discretion in enforcement (commonly known as prosecutorial or enforcement discretion); and (3) discretion in interpreting and applying statutes. In so doing, it provides notable examples of each broad type of discretion, as well as potential constraints upon the exercise of particular types of discretion.

Express Delegations of Discretionary Authority

In several instances, the INA expressly grants immigration officials some degree of discretion over aliens' eligibility for particular immigration benefits or relief, including adjustment to legal immigration status or authorization to work in the United States. These statutory delegations sometimes provide immigration officials with broad discretion to determine whether and when aliens may be eligible for particular immigration benefits. In other instances, such delegations may permit immigration officials to waive the application of a statutory requirement that would bar otherwise-qualifying aliens from obtaining particular immigration benefits or relief.

Statutory Authorization to Grant Benefits or Relief

In some instances, the INA expressly authorizes the executive branch to grant certain benefits or relief to aliens. In these instances, aliens are eligible for the benefit or relief not because Congress has given the executive branch discretion to waive restrictions that would otherwise bar the aliens from the benefit or relief, as discussed below (see "Statutory Waivers of Restrictions on Benefits or Relief"), but because Congress has affirmatively provided for certain benefits or relief to be granted. In some cases where Congress has delegated discretionary authority over a particular form of benefit or relief to immigration officials,[22] it has provided clear statutory guidance for when such authority may be exercised. In other cases, there are few, if any, express limits on the authority granted to the Executive, although some would argue that prior uses of particular authorities should serve to constrain subsequent uses of this authority.[23] The authority to grant benefits or relief can play a significant role in executive discretion as to immigration, as the examples below illustrate.

Temporary Protected Status

Temporary protected status (TPS) is a type of relief from removal that Congress has authorized the executive branch to grant to aliens who presently cannot be safely returned to their home countries. Section 244 of the INA imposes a number of conditions upon who may be granted TPS. Specifically, aliens must:

- be from a foreign state that the Department of Homeland Security (DHS) has designated due to an ongoing armed conflict; an earthquake, flood, drought, epidemic, or other environmental disaster; or other "extraordinary and temporary conditions" that prevent aliens' safe return;[24]
- have been "continuously physically present" in the United States since the effective date of their home country's most recent TPS designation;[25]
- have "continuously resided" in the United States since whatever date the executive may designate (generally a date that is earlier than the TPS designation date);[26]
- be generally admissible as an immigrant and not ineligible for TPS (e.g., have not been convicted of specified offenses);[27]
- register during the period prescribed for registration by the executive branch; and
- pay any registration fee required by the executive branch.[28]

In addition, Congress has provided that TPS is generally to be withdrawn if the alien proves to have been ineligible for such status; has not remained "continuously physically present" since the date he or she was first granted TPS; or fails "without good cause" to register annually.[29]

Despite these conditions, a grant of TPS can afford significant relief to individual aliens because aliens with TPS are provided identifying documentation and work authorization by the executive branch, and they cannot be removed while they have TPS.[30] TPS can also be a powerful tool for the Executive in crafting immigration policy. For example, TPS could be employed to enable aliens who are from countries where large numbers of persons have been displaced—and who are unlikely to qualify as refugees[31]—to remain in the United States.[32] Further, while TPS is "temporary," in practice, aliens from designated countries are often able to legally remain and work in the United States for years, potentially prompting further migration from the country.[33]

What Is the Relationship between TPS and Extended Voluntary Departure and Deferred Enforced Departure?

Legislation expressly giving the executive branch the authority to grant TPS was enacted in 1990, and is generally seen to have been in response to the Executive's prior use of extended voluntary departure (EVD) and deferred enforced departure (DED) as devices to permit aliens to avoid removal to certain countries for a period of time.

During various periods between 1960 and 1990, the executive branch granted either EVD or "nonenforcement of departure"—later known as DED—to persons from Poland, Cuba, the Dominican Republic, Czechoslovakia, Chile, Vietnam, Lebanon, Hungary, Romania, Uganda, Iran, Nicaragua, Afghanistan, Ethiopia, and China. Such grants of EVD and DED were not expressly authorized by statute, although in at least one case, Congress enacted legislation expressing its sense that the Executive ought to consider persons from a specific country (El Salvador) for EVD.

The executive branch has continued to grant DED, in particular, even after creation of TPS authority, typically to provide relief to aliens who would not qualify for TPS. For example, in 1999, President Clinton granted DED to Liberians who's TPS had expired. This grant was continued by the George W. Bush and Obama Administrations.

See generally P.L. 98-164, §1012, 97 Stat. 1062; S. HRG. 99-204; Jeanne Butterfield, Former Director, Am. Immigr. Lawyers Ass'n, et al., Memorandum, Executive Branch Authority Regarding Implementation of Immigration Laws and Policies, Apr. 29, 2011 (copy on file with the authors).

Work Authorization

Another example of discretionary authority to grant benefits or relief conferred by statute involves employment authorization documents (EADs) permitting aliens to legally work in the United States. In general, the INA provides that only specified categories of aliens are eligible to obtain employment in the United States, and INA §274A bars the hiring or continued employment of "unauthorized aliens."[34] The definition of *unauthorized alien* found in INA §274A describes an *unauthorized alien*, in part, as an alien who is not "authorized to be ... employed ... by the Attorney General [currently, the Secretary of Homeland Security]."[35] This language has generally been construed as giving immigration officials broad discretion to grant EADs to aliens, including those without lawful immigration status.[36] There are no express conditions contained in the INA regarding when the Secretary of Homeland Security may grant work authorization,[37] and the executive branch has promulgated regulations that provide for the issuance of EADs to aliens who have been granted various and often temporary forms of relief from removal, including deferred action and deferred enforced departure.[38]

Work authorization regulations promulgated by immigration agencies have played an important role in the Obama Administration's DACA initiative. Because DHS regulations had already provided for the issuance of EADs to aliens granted deferred action when such aliens establish "an economic necessity for employment,"[39] DACA beneficiaries were effectively made eligible for EADs as a corollary of receiving deferred action. Further, because many states had laws providing for the issuance of driver's licenses to aliens whose presence in the United States is "authorized" under federal law, and accepted EADs as proof that an alien's presence was so authorized, DACA beneficiaries generally also became eligible to obtain driver's licenses in the states where they were residing.[40]

Statutory Waivers of Restrictions on Benefits or Relief

In some cases, the INA provides immigration officers with discretionary authority to waive statutory requirements that would otherwise render a particular alien ineligible to receive an immigration-related benefit or form of relief. Typically, a discretionary waiver permits immigration authorities to exempt application of some, but not all, of the eligibility requirements that an alien must otherwise satisfy. Judicial review of decisions to exercise waiver authority is typically limited and, in some cases, is largely barred by statute.[41] However, federal courts may review questions of law raised by the Executive's use of waiver authority (e.g., whether immigration authorities properly found that an alien was statutorily *ineligible* for a waiver).[42]

The parameters of any waiver authority are controlled by the terms of the relevant statute, but where that statute is silent or ambiguous, the Executive could be said to have some discretion in determining how the waiver is applied. Some Members of Congress have, for example, recently suggested that the Executive expand its interpretation of what constitutes "hardship" for purposes of certain waivers, discussed below, so as to give additional unlawfully present aliens a basis for obtaining legal status in the United States.[43]

Waivers of Grounds of Inadmissibility

Arguably some of the most significant examples of discretionary waiver authority involve application of the grounds of inadmissibility listed in INA §212.[44] In general, an alien who has not been lawfully admitted into the United States is subject to exclusion or (if the alien is found at a U.S. port of entry or within the United States) removal from the country if the alien is inadmissible under INA §212.[45] Some grounds of inadmissibility constitute permanent bars to an alien's admission into the United States, such as those applicable to aliens who have committed specified criminal offenses or who have sought to procure an immigration benefit through fraud or misrepresentation.[46] In other cases, a ground of inadmissibility may bar an alien from being admitted into the United States for a certain period of time. For instance, an alien who was previously ordered removed from the United States, or who had been unlawfully present in the country for more than 180 days before departing the country, is thereafter inadmissible for a specified number of years.[47]

The INA provides immigration authorities with the ability to waive application of many of these grounds in certain situations, and thereby enable otherwise-excludable aliens to be lawfully admitted into the United States. Most notably, the immigration authorities have discretion to waive most of the inadmissibility grounds with respect to applicants for *nonimmigrant visas*, so that such aliens may be permitted to enter the United States on a temporary basis.[48] An alien who obtains such a waiver remains ineligible to receive an immigrant visa allowing him or her to come to the United States on a permanent basis, and would also be unable to adjust to LPR status while present in the United States on a nonimmigrant visa.[49]

Immigration officials may also waive certain grounds of inadmissibility so that aliens may be admitted into the United States on *immigrant visas* and/or granted adjustment to LPR status in certain instances. Examples include the following:

- INA §212(a)(9)(B)(v) permits the waiver of the inadmissibility provision applicable to aliens who have been unlawfully present in the United States for more than 180 days, if immigration authorities determine that refusing to admit the alien would result in "extreme hardship" for a U.S. citizen or LPR who is the spouse or parent of the alien.[50]
- INA §212(h) generally authorizes immigration officers to waive many of the inadmissibility grounds concerning criminal activity for qualifying aliens,[51] including those (1) whose convictions for the

criminal offenses rendering them inadmissible occurred more than 15 years before the date of the alien's application for a visa, admission, or adjustment of status, and who are deemed rehabilitated and not a threat to U.S. welfare, safety, and security; or (2) whose denial of admission would result in "extreme hardship" for a U.S. citizen or LPR who is the spouse, parent, or child of the alien.[52] However, the eligibility for waivers of aliens who had previously been admitted as LPRs and lost such status, and thereafter seek to be readmitted as LPRs or adjust to LPR status, is circumscribed.[53]

- INA §212(i) permits the waiver of the ground of inadmissibility applicable to aliens who procured or sought to procure an immigration benefit through fraud or misrepresentation,[54] when it is determined that the denial of the alien's lawful admission would result in "extreme hardship" to a U.S. citizen or LPR who is the spouse or parent of the alien.[55]
- Former INA §212(c) gave immigration officials discretion to waive most grounds of inadmissibility with respect to LPRs who had temporarily proceeded abroad and sought reentry into the United States, provided that the LPR had been domiciled in the United States at least seven years and met certain other conditions (i.e., had not served at least five years' imprisonment for an aggravated felony conviction, and was not inadmissible on grounds relating to national security or international child abduction).[56] This waiver authority had also been construed by immigration officials and reviewing courts to apply to LPRs who were present in the United States and undergoing deportation hearings.[57] Although this waiver provision was deleted from the INA in 1996, courts have construed such authority as remaining available to immigration officials with respect to resident aliens who are removable on account of guilty pleas arising prior to the repeal of INA §212(c).[58]

Hardship as a Requirement for Certain Relief from Removal

In several instances, the INA provides that, for an alien to be eligible for a particular form of relief from removal, the alien's removal must cause "hardship" to a member of the alien's immediate family who is a U.S. citizen or LPR. The nature of these hardship requirements has changed over time, and varies depending upon the particular benefit at issue.

Most of the current hardship-based waivers to the grounds of inadmissibility require that the alien's exclusion or removal would cause "extreme hardship" to an immediate family member who is a U.S. citizen or LPR. On the other hand, to qualify for cancellation of removal under INA §240A(b)(1), aliens who are not LPRs must establish that their removal would cause "exceptional and extremely unusual hardship" to a spouse, parent, or child who is a U.S. citizen or LPR.

Neither "extreme hardship" nor "exceptional and extremely unusual hardship" is defined by the INA, and both terms have been subject to varying interpretations over the years. Immigration authorities have typically construed "extreme hardship" to necessitate a showing of greater harm than typically results from an alien's removal, but the elements required to demonstrate "extreme hardship" are dependent upon the facts and particularities of each case. A nonexhaustive list of factors potentially relevant to assessing whether removal would cause "extreme hardship" to a qualifying relative include: the affected family member's ties to the United States; the conditions of the country where the qualifying relative might relocate as a result of the alien's removal, and the relative's ties to that country; the financial impact of the qualifying relative's departure from the United States in order to join the relocated alien; and the potential implications that the alien's removal would have for the qualifying relative's health. The "exceptional and extremely unusual hardship" standard used to assess aliens' eligibility for cancellation of removal under INA §240A(b)(1) has been construed to require the alien to demonstrate a greater degree of hardship than the "extreme hardship" standard, although the alien need not show such hardship is "unconscionable."

See generally 23 I. & N. Dec. 56 (BIA 2001); 22 I. & N. Dec. 560 (BIA 1999).

Parole

While not typically characterized as a waiver, INA §212(d)(5) gives immigration officials broad discretion to permit aliens to enter or remain in the United States, at least temporarily, notwithstanding the fact that the alien may otherwise be inadmissible. As previously discussed, the INA authorizes immigration officials to waive certain grounds of inadmissibility, and thereby permit excludable aliens to be admitted into the United States as immigrants or nonimmigrants. In contrast, the parole of an alien into the United States does not constitute "admission" for immigration purposes. Despite the paroled alien's physical presence in the country, the alien is "still in theory of law at the boundary line" of the United States,[59] and has not been conferred with legal immigration status. Nonetheless, some aliens who obtain parole may be able to adjust to lawful permanent resident (LPR) status while present in the United States (provided they are not covered by a ground of inadmissibility, or any applicable ground of inadmissibility is waived).[60] Aliens granted parole may also, under current regulations, be granted work authorization.[61]

The use of parole authority has been authorized by statute since the INA was originally enacted in 1952. Over the years, the statutory language concerning parole authority has been amended, but the focus has remained upon those persons whose entry into the country is deemed warranted due to emergent or humanitarian concerns, or because the alien's entry is in the public interest. The INA currently permits the Secretary of Homeland Security to parole aliens into the United States "only on a case-by-case basis for urgent humanitarian reasons or significant public benefit," and further restricts the usage of parole with respect to alien crewmembers or refugees.[62]

As noted in the text box below, parole authority has been exercised by the executive branch with respect to various groups of aliens. Most routinely, "advance parole" has been used to permit certain non-LPRs (e.g., nonimmigrants whose visa does not permit readmission; aliens who lack lawful immigration status but have been permitted to remain in the country) to reenter the United States after a brief departure.[63] "Parole-in-place" has also been granted to some unlawfully present aliens, most notably, the spouses, children, or parents of those serving, or who previously served, on active duty in the U.S. Armed Forces or the Selected Reserve of the Ready Reserve. [64] Once granted parole-in-place, such aliens are no longer seen as unlawfully present and are potentially eligible to adjust status pursuant to INA §245, as discussed below (see "Eligibility of Aliens with TPS for Adjustment of Status"). Most recently, some commentators have suggested that the Executive could make greater use of parole and parole-in-place to facilitate the entry of more nonimmigrant workers, or permit immediate relatives of U.S. citizens or LPRs to legalize their status.[65]

A Brief History of the Executive Branch's Parole of Aliens into the United States

The executive branch's practice of paroling excludable or inadmissible aliens into the United States dates back to the early 1900s, when immigration officials adopted the practice to avoid holding aliens in custody pending their exclusion.

Parole was also used to permit aliens to remain in the United States for a period of time when "the case was exceptionally meritorious and immediate deportation would be inhumane."

When the INA was adopted in 1952, it provided express statutory authority for this executive branch practice, permitting aliens applying for admission to be paroled into the United States "temporarily under such conditions as [the Executive] may prescribe for emergent reasons or for reasons deemed strictly in the public interest." The legislative history suggests that the INA's drafters intended the parole authority to be used only in limited circumstances. The initial draft of the INA reportedly would have restricted parole to aliens requiring medical treatment in the United States. Although the language adopted was not so narrow, the drafters seem to have envisioned parole being used to permit aliens to enter only for "immediate medical attention," or as "a witness or for purposes of prosecution." Subsequent statements of members of the drafting committee support this view, emphasizing that the drafters envisioned parole as applying in "unique individual cases" on a "temporary and at best conditional basis."

The executive branch, however, used its parole authority under the INA more broadly. For example, the 1953 INS annual report notes the parole into the United States of 386 natives of Estonia, Latvia, Finland, Sweden, Poland, and the Soviet Union who had initially sought refuge from Russian Communists in Sweden, and then sailed to various U.S. ports between 1945 and 1950.

A subsequent Senate report similarly notes the parole of 925 orphans from Eastern Europe in 1956; 38,045 refugees from Hungary in 1957; 19,754 refugees from Eastern Europe in 1960-1965; 14,741 Chinese refugees from Hong Kong and Macao in 1962; 692,219 refugees from Cuba in 1962-1979; 35,758 refugees from the Soviet Union in 1973-1979; 208,200 Indochinese refugees in 1975-1979; 1,422 Chileans in 1975-1977; another 343 Latin Americans in 1976-1977; an estimated 1,000 Lebanese in 1978-1979; and an estimated 15,000 Cuban prisoners and family members in 1979.

Later, although parole was arguably less common, it was still used with Jewish persons from the Soviet Union in 1988-1989; certain Haitians interdicted at sea and detained at Guantanamo who had medical conditions in 1991-1992; and Haitian orphans in 2010. These grants of parole generally reflected humanitarian concerns tied to the aliens' situations.

However, domestic labor needs were sometimes taken into account when granting parole, as happened when Hong Kong Chinese were selected for parole based, in part, on their "possessing special skills needed in the United States" and 2,468 aliens were paroled into Guam to "support defense projects" following a typhoon.

In some instances, Congress pushed back against the executive branch's broad use of its parole authority, as when a 1965 committee report stated that "it is the express intent of the committee that the parole provisions ... be administered in accordance with the original intention of the drafters ... The parole provisions were designed to authorize the Attorney General to act only in emergent, individual, and isolated situations, such as the case of an alien who requires immediate medical attention, and not for the immigration of classes or groups outside of the limit of the law." However, in other cases, Congress responded to the executive branch's granting of parole to groups of refugees by enacting legislation which permitted parolees to become LPRs (e.g., P.L. 85-559 (Hungarian parolees); P.L. 89-732 (Cuban parolees)). In addition, in 1960, Congress enacted legislation (P.L. 86-648) that could be seen as having ratified (at least for a time) the executive branch's use of parole to admit refugees by temporarily authorizing the use of parole for this purpose.

See generally INS Annual Reports for 1949, 1950, 1962, and 1963; 2 U.S.C.C.A.N. 1653, 1706 (1952); S. REP. NO. 748, 89th Cong., 1st Sess. at 16-17; H.R. REP. NO. 96-814, at 88; S. REP. NO. 256, 96th Cong., 2d Sess. at 6; Soviet Refugees: Hearing, 101st Cong., 1st Sess. (1989); 27 Geo. Wash. L. Rev. 373, 374 n. 11 (1959); 16 IN DEFENSE OF THE ALIEN 135 (1993); 55 N.Y. L. SCH. L. REV. 791 (2010).

Potential Constraints

As these examples suggest, exercises of affirmative authority to grant benefits or relief, or to waive restrictions on benefits or relief, must be consistent with any statutory limitations. For example, the Executive is arguably barred from considering "hardship" to the alien, or to the alien's children, in determining whether to waive the three- and 10-year bars upon the admissibility of aliens who have accrued at least 180 days of unlawful presence in the United States because INA §212(a)(9)(B)(v) expressly refers to waivers:

> in the case of an immigrant who is the spouse or son or daughter of a United States citizen or of an alien lawfully admitted for permanent residence, if it is established ... that the refusal of admission to such [an] alien would result in extreme hardship to the citizen or lawfully resident spouse or parent of such alien.[66]

However, in cases where the INA is silent or ambiguous, the Executive could potentially have more discretion as to how affirmative authority to grant benefits or relief, or waive restrictions on benefits or relief, is exercised. (See "Discretion in Interpreting and Applying Statutes.")

In addition, even where there are few, if any, statutory restrictions upon the Executive's ability to grant immigration-related benefits or relief, questions might be raised about whether particular exercises of authority are consistent with historical practice, other provisions of the INA, or Congress's intent in granting the executive branch specific authority. For example, while nothing in the INA expressly prohibits the executive branch from doing so, granting EADs to every alien who comes to the United States, regardless of such alien's legal status, would be unprecedented.[67] Similarly, if the Executive hypothetically were to propose granting work authorization to all aliens coming to the United States, an argument could be made that doing so would be inconsistent with the provisions that Congress made in the INA for the protection of domestic labor in the granting of employment-based immigrant and nonimmigrant visas.[68] An argument could also be made that Congress is unlikely to have defined *unauthorized alien* and prohibited the knowing hiring or employment of such aliens if it contemplated the executive branch granting work authorization to all aliens.

DISCRETION IN ENFORCEMENT

The Executive is generally recognized as possessing some degree of independent authority in assessing when, against whom, how, and even whether to prosecute apparent violations of federal law; an authority generally referred to as "prosecutorial discretion" or "enforcement discretion."[69] It is generally recognized that the executive branch may exercise prosecutorial or enforcement discretion in the field of immigration,[70] including in determining:

- whether to commence removal proceedings and the nature of the particular charges to lodge against an alien;[71]

- whether to cancel a Notice to Appear (NTA) or other charging document before jurisdiction vests with an immigration judge;[72] and
- whether to appeal an immigration judge's decision or order.[73]

The granting of immigration benefits, in contrast, has historically been seen not as an exercise of prosecutorial or enforcement discretion inherent to the executive branch, but as an exercise of authority expressly delegated by Congress.[74]

The exercise of prosecutorial or enforcement discretion in specific cases has historically been based on humanitarian factors,[75] and/or resources constraints.[76] A "favorable" exercise of discretion (e.g., one permitting a potentially removable alien to remain in the United States) generally does not grant the alien legal status, despite the alien having legal permission to remain in the country.[77] However, by enabling the alien to remain in the United States, a favorable exercise of discretion could permit the alien to acquire a basis for legalization in the future (e.g., the establishment of ties that would provide a basis for adjustment of status under current law, or following the enactment of a legalization measure like the Immigration Reform and Control Act of 1986).[78]

Determining Whether to Issue an NTA

One example of the Executive's prosecutorial or enforcement discretion as to immigration involves determinations as to whether to issue Notices to Appear (NTAs) or other charging documents initiating proceedings against individual aliens who are believed to be removable.[79] Such discretion has likely been used as long as there have been grounds for deporting or removing aliens, with individual immigration officers determining that humanitarian factors or resource constraints were such that action against specific individuals was not warranted. A few "large scale" examples have also been noted, such as the then-INS's determination in 1962 to permit "56,800 refugee overstay visitors [from Cuba] ... to remain in the United States for an indefinite period," rather than seeking their removal.[80] (These persons were apparently separate and apart from the 62,500 Cuban parolees, and the 6,500 Cubans in visitor status, also reported that year as having been permitted to remain in the United States indefinitely).[81]

However, there is only sporadic evidence regarding such uses of discretion until the mid-1970s, when the executive branch began issuing memoranda that elaborated on specific aspects of immigration enforcement and, particularly, its practices and priorities as to immigration enforcement. Currently, for example, these memoranda establish a general policy of not engaging in arrests, interviews, searches, or surveillance for purely immigration enforcement purposes near schools or churches.[82] Conversely, the "highest priority" is given to the removal of:

> aliens engaged in or suspected of terrorism or espionage, or who otherwise pose a danger to national security; aliens convicted of crimes, with a particular emphasis on violent criminals, felons, and repeat offenders; aliens not younger than 16 who participated in organized criminal gangs; aliens subject to outstanding criminal warrants; and aliens who otherwise pose a serious risk to public safety.[83]

Some have recently called for changes to the executive branch guidance regarding the issuance of NTAs and, in particular, the cessation of the Secure Communities program.[84] Secure Communities relies upon information sharing between various levels and agencies of government to identify potentially removable aliens,[85] and critics have alleged that the program has resulted in the removal of aliens who are not priorities for removal under the DHS guidance quoted above.[86]

Deferred Action

Another example of discretion in enforcing immigration law involves the granting of deferred action to removable aliens.[87] Grants of deferred action date back to at least the 1970s,[88] and are distinct from determinations not to issue NTAs or take other enforcement action. Generally, there is no record of an immigration officer's determination not to issue an NTA, and one immigration officer's determination not to issue an NTA to an individual alien is generally not seen as "binding" on other officers encountering the same alien. The situation is different as to grants of deferred action, which are documented in the alien's immigration file (commonly known as the "A file"), and have historically been seen to govern unless and until there are changes in the alien's circumstances.[89]

Immigration officials may grant deferred action on their own initiative, or aliens can request deferred action if they know it is an option. The Obama Administration's DACA initiative is perhaps the best known example of deferred action, although it arguably differs from other grants of deferred action in that the ability to request relief is widely known and the factors considered in granting it are explicit.[90] Additionally, grants of deferred action through DACA last for two years, with the possibility of renewal, as opposed to being open-ended like grants of deferred action outside DACA generally are.[91] Some have also said that grants of deferred action through DACA are different in that DACA applies to a "category" of aliens.[92] However, determinations as to whether to grant deferred action through DACA are made on an individual basis,[93] and the Obama Administration has repeatedly stated that no one is entitled to deferred action through DACA, not even if all "the guidelines [suggesting the alien warrants a favorable exercise of discretion] are met."[94] The Administration has also continued to grant deferred action to aliens outside the DACA initiative, although on a smaller scale.[95] Some have recently called for the extension of DACA, or a DACA-type program, for other aliens, although proposals as to which aliens should be granted deferred action through such a program have varied (e.g., parents of U.S. citizens, aliens eligible to legalize under S. 744, 113th Cong.).[96]

Potential Constraints

The executive branch's enforcement discretion is subject to two notable limits, neither of which is necessarily judicially enforceable.[97] The first is that the express adoption of a policy that constitutes an abdication of a statutory duty could be found to be impermissible under the rationale articulated by the Supreme Court in its 1985 decision in *Heckler v. Cheney*. The *Heckler* Court expressly recognized the possibility of an executive agency "consciously and expressly adopt[ing] a general policy [of not enforcing the law] that is so extreme as to amount to an abdication of its statutory responsibilities." [98] However, the *Heckler* Court did not elaborate upon what might constitute such an abdication,[99] and at least one federal court of appeals subsequently took the view that "[r]eal or perceived inadequate enforcement ... does not constitute a reviewable abdication of duty."[100] Instead, the appellate court opined that the plaintiffs must show that the Executive either is "doing nothing to enforce the ... laws," or has "consciously decided to abdicate" its enforcement responsibilities.[101]

Does DACA Constitute an Abdication of Duty?

Some have suggested that, with DACA, the Executive has essentially adopted a general policy which is in effect an abdication of its statutory duty insofar as 1.76 million aliens are potentially eligible for relief from removal under DACA. However, the fact that a prosecutorial discretion policy favorably affects a large number of people may not – in and of itself – amount to an abdication of a statutory duty. Courts might also consider the size of the total population against whom the law could be enforced, as well as the resources available for enforcing the law, on the theory that "the President cannot secure full execution of the laws, if Congress denies to him adequate means of doing so." Myers v. United States, 272 U.S. 52, 291-92 (1926) (Brandeis, J., dissenting).

The existence of multiple—and sometimes inconsistent—enforcement mandates from Congress might also factor into a court's analysis of whether nonenforcement policies constitute an abdication of duty, particularly in situations where an agency elects to concentrate limited resources upon offenders (or offenses) that Congress has indicated are a priority. For example, following the enactment of the Illegal Immigration Reform and Immigrant Responsibility Act of 1996, which some assert amended the INA to require the removal of at least some unauthorized aliens, Congress enacted a number of measures directing DHS to give priority to the removal of "criminal aliens." *See, e.g.*, 125 Stat. 950; 123 Stat. 2142; 122 Stat. 3659; 121 Stat. 2050-2051. DHS has emphasized that its diminished focus on the removal of DACA-eligible individuals corresponds to an increased focus on criminal aliens, and a reviewing court could potentially find that enforcement of later-enacted mandates (as to criminal aliens) may justify more limited enforcement of earlier enacted mandates (as to unauthorized aliens generally).

The second limitation involves the view that statutes using "shall" invariably require agency action. Some statutes using "shall" have been construed in this way.[102] Perhaps most notably, a federal district court recently found that immigration officers are required to place all aliens who have not been admitted to the United States into removal proceedings because of the use of "shall" in three purportedly "interlocking provisions" in INA §235.[103] These provisions state that:

1) any alien present in the United States who has not been admitted shall be deemed an applicant for admission;
2) applicants for admission shall be inspected by immigration officers; and
3) in the case of an alien who is an applicant for admission, if the examining immigration officer determines that an alien seeking admission is not clearly and beyond a doubt entitled to be admitted, the alien shall be detained for removal proceedings.[104]

Thus, the district court concluded that DACA runs afoul of the INA because many of the aliens granted deferred action through DACA had never been placed in removal proceedings as required, in the court's view, by INA §235. (This same court, however, later ruled that it lacked jurisdiction over the case.[105] That decision has been appealed, and it is presently unclear whether and how its earlier decision construing INA §235 could be seen to restrain any future grants of deferred action.[106]) On the other hand, not all statutes using "shall" have been construed to eliminate executive discretion, particularly not in cases where the statute prescribes that persons be sanctioned for particular violations.[107] For example, in a 2011 decision, the Board of Immigration Appeals (BIA), the highest administrative body for construing and applying immigration law, found that immigration officers have discretion as to whether to pursue expedited removal proceedings under INA §235 or formal removal proceedings under INA §240, notwithstanding the fact that the INA uses "shall" in describing who is subject to expedited removal.[108] In so doing, the BIA specifically noted that:

> in the Federal criminal code, Congress has defined most crimes by providing that whoever engages in certain conduct "shall" be imprisoned or otherwise punished. But this has never been construed to require a Federal prosecutor to bring charges against every person believed to have violated the statute.[109]

Who Has Standing to Challenge Exercises of Enforcement Discretion?

Standing requirements are concerned with who is a proper party to seek judicial relief from a federal court. Standing requirements derive from Article III of the Constitution, which confines the jurisdiction of federal courts to actual "Cases" and "Controversies."

The case-or-controversy requirement has long been construed to restrict Article III courts to the adjudication of real, live disputes involving parties who have "a personal stake in the outcome of the controversy." Parties seeking judicial relief from an Article III court must generally show three things in order to demonstrate standing: (1) they have suffered an "injury in fact" that is (a) concrete and particularized and (b) actual or imminent; (2) the injury is fairly traceable to the challenged action of the defendant; and (3) the injury is likely to be redressed by a favorable decision.

Standing can be difficult to show in cases involving an Executive's policy or practice of not enforcing the law in particular cases. Those whose sole injury is the government's alleged failure to follow the law will generally be found to lack standing because this injury is not personal and particularized.

Government officers and employees, who have taken an oath to uphold the law, will also generally be found to lack standing so long as their only asserted injury is being forced to violate their oaths by implementing an allegedly unlawful policy or practice. Instead, they must allege some separate and concrete adverse consequence that would flow from violating their oath, and courts have reached differing conclusions as to whether the possibility of being disciplined for obeying—or refusing to obey—allegedly unlawful orders suffices for purposes of standing, or whether such injury is "entirely speculative" and, therefore, lacking imminence. In the case of the ICE officers who brought suit to challenge the Obama Administration's DACA initiative, the reviewing district court found that the plaintiffs had standing because of the possibility of such discipline. However, because such discipline constitutes an adverse employment action, this court subsequently found that the plaintiff's case is within the jurisdiction of the Merit Systems Protection Board, rather than that of the court.

Individual Members of Congress also generally lack standing to challenge presidential actions. In *Raines v. Byrd*, the Supreme Court held that in order to obtain standing an individual Member must assert either a personal injury, like the loss of his or her congressional seat, or an institutional injury which cannot be addressed by an extant legislative remedy.

See CRS Report R42924, *Prosecutorial Discretion in Immigration Enforcement: Legal Issues*, by Kate M. Manuel and Todd Garvey; CRS Report R43712, *Article III Standing and Congressional Suits Against the Executive Branch*, by Alissa M. Dolan.

DISCRETION IN INTERPRETING AND APPLYING STATUTES

Another type of discretion that the executive branch may exercise as to immigration law involves the interpretation and application of statutes. As the Supreme Court articulated in its 1984 decision in *Chevron U.S.A. v. Natural Resources Defense Council*, when "Congress has directly spoken to the issue, ... that is the end of the matter; for the court, as well as the agency, must give effect to the unambiguously expressed intent of Congress."[110] However, where a statute is "silent or ambiguous with respect to a specific issue," courts will generally defer to an agency interpretation that is based on a "permissible construction of the statute,"[111] on the grounds that the executive branch must fill any "gaps" implicitly or explicitly left by Congress in the course of administering congressional programs.[112] The degree of deference afforded to particular executive branch interpretations can vary depending upon the facts and circumstances of the case, including whether the interpretation is a "formal" one adopted through notice-and-comment rulemaking or case-by-case adjudication.[113] There are a number of places where the INA is silent or ambiguous on particular issues, and the executive branch has—expressly or practically—adopted an interpretation that significantly affects the implementation of immigration law. As some commentators have suggested,[114] these executive branch interpretations could potentially be changed to expand (or restrict) aliens' ability to enter or remain in the United States without the enactment of additional legislation.

Not Counting Derivatives

One recently proposed change in the Executive's interpretation of the INA involves the counting of so-called "derivatives"—or noncitizen spouses or children of alien beneficiaries of family- or employment-based visa petitions, who are not themselves the subject of such petitions.[115] Derivatives can immigrate with the so-called "principal" whom they accompany,[116] but the INA does not expressly address whether derivatives are to be counted against the annual caps on the number of immigrants (other than "immediate relatives" of U.S. citizens) who may be admitted to the United States each year. Section 203(d) of INA states only that:

> A spouse or child as defined in subparagraph (A), (B), (C), (D), or (E) of section 1101(b)(1) of this title shall, if not otherwise entitled

> to an immigrant status and the immediate issuance of a visa under subsection (a), (b), or (c) of this section, be entitled to the same status, and the same order of consideration provided in the respective subsection, if accompanying or following to join, the spouse or parent.[117]

The executive branch has historically counted derivatives against the annual caps on the number of immigrants, with the result that 78,089 of the 143,998 total employment-based immigrant visas issued in FY2012 reportedly went to derivatives.[118] Because the counting of derivatives can thus be seen as diminishing the number of aliens who may immigrate each year for employment reasons, and as delaying family-based immigration, some have recently suggested that the executive branch cease counting derivatives against the annual caps as a way to permit additional employment- or family-based immigration without congressional action (e.g., the adoption of legislation increasing the annual caps provided in INA §201).[119] Other provisions of the INA could, however, potentially be said to be inconsistent with such an interpretation,[120] and might factor into any Executive determination as to whether to adopt this interpretation.

Eligibility of Aliens with TPS for Adjustment of Status

Another recently proposed change in the executive branch's interpretation of the INA concerns whether aliens granted TPS under INA §244 are eligible for adjustment of status under INA §245.[121] Section 245 permits adjustment of status for aliens who were "inspected and admitted or paroled" and are "admissible for permanent residence," among other things.[122] However, the executive branch has historically taken the view that aliens granted TPS are neither "admitted or paroled" nor "admissible" as those terms are defined by INA §101.[123] Thus, in DHS's longstanding view, they are ineligible for adjustment of status.

On the other hand, neither INA §245 nor INA §101 expressly addresses whether unlawfully present aliens granted TPS are eligible for adjustment of status or are admitted/admissible, and a draft memorandum sent by several USCIS employees to the Director of USCIS in 2010 noted that changing DHS's interpretation to permit adjustment of status under INA §245 for aliens with TPS would "promote family unity" and "reduce the threat of removal for certain individuals present in the United States without authorization."[124] DHS has generally not adopted such an interpretation to date. However, it has adopted the interpretation within the territorial jurisdiction of the U.S. Court of Appeals for the Seventh Circuit[125] following a 2013 decision wherein that court found that INA §244—which governs the granting of TPS—requires that those with TPS be seen as admissible.[126]

Potential Constraints

Although these examples illustrate that the executive branch may have some discretion in interpreting and applying immigration law when the INA is silent or ambiguous on particular issues, this discretion is not unlimited. As previously noted, the executive branch's interpretation may be constrained if Congress has directly spoken to the precise question at issue.[127] Moreover, even if Congress has not spoken on the question, the executive branch's interpretation must still be seen as constituting a "permissible" and "reasonable" interpretation of the underlying statute in order to be afforded deference by the courts.[128]

How Does the Executive Branch Change Its Interpretation?

How the executive branch changes its interpretation of an immigration statute depends, in part, upon the degree of formality surrounding the issuance of its current interpretation. There are two primary ways to change *formal interpretations* (i.e., regulations, adjudication). One involves the promulgation of changes to regulations through notice-and comment rulemaking. Such rulemaking can be expedited in limited circumstances (e.g., direct final rules, interim final rules). Alternatively, a BIA decision could be certified to the Attorney General (AG).

DOJ regulations implementing the INA, rather than the INA itself, provide for the *certification* of BIA decisions to the AG for his review. Specifically, these regulations require that the Board refer to the AG for review all cases that: (i) the AG directs the Board to refer; (ii) the Chairman or a majority of the BIA believes should be referred; or (iii) the Secretary of Homeland Security, or specific DHS officials designated by the Secretary with the concurrence of the AG, refers for review. These regulations also require that the decisions of the AG in certified cases be in writing and transmitted to the BIA or DHS for forwarding to the aliens or parties affected.

However, the regulations impose no other requirements, leaving the AG with discretion to certify any BIA decision he wishes, and to address any issues he chooses in a decision that is certified to him. Historical example suggests that the BIA decisions which are certified to the Attorney General need not be published or precedential ones, and that their certification to the Attorney General may occur many months after the BIA decision. In addition, prior AGs have characterized their power of review in certified cases as "plenary", in that they may engage in *de novo* review of law and facts, unconstrained by the regulations that bind the BIA in their consideration of cases.

Informal interpretations are generally more quickly and easily changed, for example, by withdrawing or modifying informal guidance. For example, in January 2014, the Department of State (DOS) announced changes in its interpretation of the term *parent* in INA §§301& 309, which govern the acquisition of citizenship at birth for persons born abroad. It did so through a policy memorandum noting that it had formerly construed *parent* to require there be a genetic link between the U.S. citizen parent(s) and the child, but would hereafter recognize gestational ties as well. DHS subsequently announced the issuance of a similar policy in October 2014.

See generally 8 C.F.R. §1003.1(h)(1)(i)-(iii) & (2); *Matter of* J-S-, 24 I. & N. Dec. 520, 531 (AG 2008); *Matter of* D-J-, 23 I. & N. Dec. 572, 575 (AG 2003).

Concerns could also be raised about the deference to be accorded to new agency interpretations that are inconsistent with a long-standing interpretation of the agency, particularly an interpretation that third-parties have relied upon. The Supreme Court rejected the view that "inconsistency" in agency regulations is a "basis for declining to analyze the agency's interpretation under the *Chevron* framework" in its 2005 decision in *National Cable & Telecommunications Association v. Brand X Internet Services.*[129] However, in so doing, it noted that any "[u]nexplained inconsistency" could be a "reason for holding a regulatory interpretation to be an arbitrary and capricious change from agency practice under the Administrative Procedure Act."[130] More recently, questions have been raised about changes in certain informal interpretations of agency regulations. Several federal courts of appeals have found that agencies cannot substantively change rules interpreting agency regulations that parties have relied upon without providing formal public notice and requesting comment under the APA.[131] Other courts have adopted a different view,[132] and the Supreme Court is scheduled to hear oral arguments on the issue in December 2014.[133]

Some may also argue that certain executive actions as to immigration implicate the "major policy" exception to the general principle of *Chevron* deference in cases where the Executive's interpretation could be said to mark a significant change in policy that Congress arguably did not directly contemplate. Such an exception is generally grounded in the Supreme Court's statement, in its 2000 decision in *FDA v. Brown & Williamson* that "Congress could not have intended to delegate a decision of such economic and political significance [as whether to regulate tobacco pursuant to delegated authority to regulate 'drugs'] to an agency."[134] The *Brown & Williamson* Court also suggested there may be reason to deny deference in all "extraordinary cases" that involve "major questions."[135] However, the Supreme Court's 2007 decision in *Massachusetts v. EPA* is generally seen to have limited, if not vitiated, the "major policy" exception by requiring the Executive to implement an arguably major policy adopted by the Environmental Protection Agency through regulations rather than by statute.[136]

End Notes

[1] White House, Office of the Press Secretary, Remarks by the President on Border Security and Immigration Reform, June 30, 2014, *available at* http://www.whitehouse.gov/the-press-office/2014/06/30/remarks-president-border-securityand-immigration-reform.

[2] Assoc. Press, *Obama, Defiant, Vows Immigration Action This Year*, WASH. POST, Nov. 5, 2014, *available at* http://www.washingtonpost.com/politics/congress/obama-firm-on-vow-to-act-on-immigration-this-year/2014/11/05/af658b1c-652a-11e4-ab86-46000e1d0035_story.html.

[3] *See, e.g., Depending on Specifics, Executive Action Could Impact Millions, MPI Report Estimates*, 8 WORKPLACE IMMIGR. REP. 606 (Sept. 11, 2014) (discussing report, Executive Action for Unauthorized Immigrants, cited *infra* note 96); *Obama Said to Be Developing Plans to Give Millions Work Authorization*, 8 WORKPLACE IMMIGR. REP. 518 (Aug. 4, 2014).

[4] *See* Dept. of Homeland Security (DHS), U.S. Citizenship & Immigr. Servs. (USCIS), Number of I-821D, Consideration of Deferred Action for Childhood Arrivals by Fiscal Year, Quarter, Intake, Biometrics and Case Status: 2012-2014, *available at* http://www.uscis.gov/sites/default/files/USCIS/Resources/Reports%20and%20Studies/Immigration%20Forms%20Data/All%20Form%20Types/DACA/DACA_fy2014_qtr3.pdf (last accessed: Oct. 27, 2014).

[5] *See, e.g.*, Shoba Sivaprasad Wadhia, *In Defense of DACA, Deferred Action, and the DREAM Act*, 91 TEX. L. REV. 59 (2013) (responding to arguments raised by Delahunty & Yoo, *infra*, note 6, and claiming that DACA is a constitutionally justified attempt by the Executive "to enforce congressionally mandated priorities" by focusing limited resources on

the removal of aliens designated as a "high-priority" for removal); David A. Martin, *A Defense of Immigration-Enforcement Discretion: The Legal and Policy Flaws of Kris Kobach's Latest Crusade*, 122 YALE L.J. ONLINE 167 (2012) (arguing that DACA is consistent with the INA and with previous exercises of enforcement discretion by immigration officials).

[6] *See, e.g.,* Crane v. Napolitano, Amended Complaint, No. 3:12-cv-03247-O, filed Oct. 10, 2012 (N.D. Tex.) (lawsuit challenging DACA and arguing that the initiative is, among other things, contrary to certain provisions of the INA and the Executive's constitutional responsibility to take care that the laws are faithfully executed); Robert J. Delahunty & John C. Yoo, *Dream On: The Obama Administration's Nonenforcement of Immigration Laws, the DREAM Act, and the Take Care Clause*, 91 TEX. L. REV. 781 (2013) (arguing that the DACA initiative is inconsistent with the Executive's constitutional duties, and that the President may not purposefully refrain from enforcing federal statutes against broad categories of persons "in ordinary, noncritical circumstances").

[7] The INA is codified in 8 U.S.C. §1101 *et seq.*

[8] Certain conduct by aliens who have not been lawfully admitted into the United States renders them inadmissible and, if found physically present within the United States, subject to removal. INA §212, 8 U.S.C. §1182. Aliens who have been lawfully admitted into the country may be subject to removal if they engage in specified conduct rendering them deportable. INA §237, 8 U.S.C. §1227.

[9] *See generally* CRS Legal Sidebar WSLG563, *An Overview of Immigration-Related Crimes*, by Michael John Garcia.

[10] *See* Arizona v. United States,—U.S.—, 132 S. Ct. 2492, 2499 (2012) ("A principal feature of the removal system is the broad discretion exercised by immigration officials. ... Federal officials, as an initial matter, must decide whether it makes sense to pursue removal at all. If removal proceedings commence, aliens may seek asylum and other discretionary relief allowing them to remain in the country or at least to leave without formal removal.").

[11] *See, e.g.,* INA §212(a)(9)(B)(v), 8 U.S.C. §1182(a)(9)(B)(v) (authorizing waiver of the ground of inadmissibility applicable to aliens unlawfully present for more than 180 days in specified circumstances); INA §212(h), 8 U.S.C. §1182(h) (conferring authority to waive many of the grounds of inadmissibility concerning criminal conduct).

[12] Asylum is a discretionary form of relief from removal available to qualifying aliens who are unable or unwilling to return to their home countries due to a well-founded fear of persecution on account of race, religion, nationality, political opinion, or membership in a particular social group. Aliens who are granted asylum may be eligible to work in the United States and adjust to lawful permanent resident (LPR) status. INA §§208, 209(b), 8 U.S.C. §§1158, 1159(b).

[13] Temporary protected status (TPS) is a "temporary" form of relief from removal that the Secretary of Homeland Security may grant to nationals from a specific country due to an ongoing crisis in that country. Aliens who are granted TPS are generally eligible to work in the United States so long as they have TPS. INA §244, 8 U.S.C. §1254a.

[14] Under INA §240A, the Attorney General is authorized to cancel the removal and adjust the status of otherwise inadmissible or deportable aliens who satisfy specified criteria (e.g., having been present or resided in the country for a specified period). *See* 8 U.S.C. §1229b. No more than 4,000 aliens may be granted such relief in any fiscal year. Aliens who were subject to removal or committed a criminal offense making them removable *prior* to the enactment of the current cancellation of removal statute may be eligible for earlier forms of

relief (suspension of deportation or a "§212(c) waiver," discussed, *infra*, at page 10), which are not subject to these numerical limitations.

[15] *See generally* CRS Report R42924, *Prosecutorial Discretion in Immigration Enforcement: Legal Issues*, by Kate M. Manuel and Todd Garvey.

[16] *See, e.g.*, DHS, U.S. Immigration and Customs Enforcement (ICE) Director John Morton, Memorandum, Exercising Prosecutorial Discretion Consistent with the Civil Immigration Enforcement Priorities of the Agency for the Apprehension, Detention, and Removal of Aliens, June 17, 2011 (copy on file with the authors) (discussing the usage of prosecutorial or enforcement discretion by immigration officials, and identifying priorities that ICE agents should consider in the exercise of such discretion).

[17] *See generally* INA §236(c), 8 U.S.C. §1226(c).

[18] Heckler v. Cheney, 470 U.S. 821, 832-833 n.4 (1985) ("Nor do we have a situation where it could justifiably be found that the agency has 'consciously and expressly adopted a general policy' that is so extreme as to amount to an abdication of its statutory responsibilities.") (citing *Adams v. Richardson*, 480 F.2d 1159 (1973) (en banc)).

[19] *See* Chevron U.S.A. v. Natural Resources Defense Council, 467 U.S. 837, 842-843 (1984) ("[When] Congress has directly spoken to the issue, ... that is the end of the matter; for the court, as well as the agency, must give effect to the unambiguously expressed intent of Congress." However, where a statute is "silent or ambiguous with respect to a specific issue," courts will generally defer to an agency interpretation that is based on a "permissible construction of the statute."). *See also* INS v. Aguirre-Aguirre, 526 U.S. 415, 424 (1999) ("It is clear that principles of *Chevron* deference are applicable" to immigration agencies' interpretation of INA requirements).

[20] *See, e.g.*, INA §212(a)(9)(B)(v), (h), & (*i*), 8 U.S.C. §1182(a)(9)(B)(v), (h), & (*i*) (authorizing waiver of specified grounds of inadmissibility when the alien's removal would cause "extreme hardship" to certain family members who are U.S. citizens or LPRs); INA §240A(b)(1)(D), 8 U.S.C. §1229b(b)(1)(D) (permitting cancellation of the removal of certain aliens whose removal would cause "exceptional and extremely unusual hardship" to certain family members who are U.S. citizens or LPRs).

[21] The Executive has, for example, construed provisions in INA §235 which some assert require that unlawfully present aliens be placed in removal proceedings as applying only to "arriving aliens," and not to aliens who are present within the country without inspection. *See* Dep't of Justice (DOJ), Immigr. & Naturalization Serv. (INS), Inspection and Expedited Removal of Aliens; Detention and Removal of Aliens; Conduct of Removal Proceedings; Asylum Procedures, 62 Fed. Reg. 10312, 10357 (Mar. 6, 1997) (codified at 8 C.F.R. §235.3(c)). *See also* DOJ, INS, Inspection and Expedited Removal of Aliens; Detention and Removal of Aliens; Conduct of Removal Proceedings; Asylum Procedures, 62 Fed. Reg. 444, 444-46 (Jan. 3, 1997) (noting that the INA "distinguishes between the broader term 'applicants for admission' and a narrower group, 'arriving aliens'"). *See* "Deferred Action" for further discussion of INA §235.

[22] Not every INA provision concerning the conferral of benefits or relief is discretionary in nature. *See, e.g.*, INA §241(b)(3), 8 U.S.C. §1231(b)(3) (generally barring removal of qualifying aliens to countries where the alien's life or freedom would be threatened because of the alien's race, religion, nationality, political opinion, or membership in a particular social group). Discussion of such mandatory forms of benefits or relief is beyond the scope of this report.

[23] *See* discussion *infra* "Potential Constraints."

[24] In the case of natural disasters, INA §244 further requires "substantial, but temporary," disruption of living conditions in the affected area, and the foreign state must be temporarily unable to handle the return of its nationals and request TPS designation. INA §244(b)(1)(B)(i), 8 U.S.C. §1254a(b)(1)(B)(i). Pursuant to INA §244, country designations must be published in the *Federal Register*, and may be for periods of no less than six months and no more than 18 months. INA §244(b)(1)-(2), 8 U.S.C. §1254a(b)(1)-(2). These designations must be reviewed at least 60 days before they expire, at which point, they may be extended if the conditions that gave rise to the designation persist. Otherwise, INA §244 requires that the designation be terminated. INA §244(b)(3)(A)-(B), 8 U.S.C. §1254a(b)(3)(A)- (B).

[25] There is an exception for "brief, casual, and innocent absences." *See* INA §244(c)(4), 8 U.S.C. §1254a(c)(4).

[26] *See, e.g.*, DHS, USCIS, Extension of the Designation of El Salvador for Temporary Protected Status, 78 Fed. Reg. 32418 (May 30, 2013) (establishing a TPS designation date of March 9, 2001, and a date of continuous residence of February 13, 2001).

[27] *See* INA §244(c)(2)(A)-(B), 8 U.S.C. §1254a(c)(2)(A)-(B). Certain grounds of inadmissibility are, however, waived for aliens seeking TPS. *Id.*

[28] INA §244(c), 8 U.S.C. §1254a(c).

[29] INA §244(c)(3), 8 U.S.C. §1254a(c)(3).

[30] INA §244(a)(1), 8 U.S.C. §1254a(a)(1) (nonremoval and work authorization); INA §244(d), 8 U.S.C. §1254a(d) (documentation).

[31] In order to qualify as a "refugee" under the INA, an alien must have experienced past persecution, or have a well-founded fear of future persecution on account of race, religion, nationality, political opinion, or membership in a particular social group. INA §101(a)(42), 8 U.S.C. §1101(a)(42). Accordingly, aliens who fear generalized lawlessness and violence in a country generally do not qualify as "refugees" under the INA.

[32] *See, e.g.*, DHS, USCIS, Extension of the Designation of Somalia for Temporary Protected Status, 78 Fed. Reg. 65690 (Nov. 1, 2013) (noting that Somalia was initially designated for TPS on September 16, 1991, "based on extraordinary and temporary conditions resulting from armed conflict").

[33] Certain aliens from Honduras have had TPS since 1999, while some from El Salvador have had it since 2001. *See* USCIS, Temporary Protected Status, Oct. 16, 2014, *available at* http://www.uscis.gov/humanitarian/temporaryprotected-status-deferred-enforced-departure/temporary-protected-status. The parents of some unaccompanied alien children (UACs) recently apprehended at the U.S. border with Mexico are present in the United States pursuant to TPS. *See, e.g.*, Donald Kerwin, *The Migration of Unaccompanied Children to the United States: Stumbling Towards a Humanitarian Solution*, HUFFINGTON POST, July 20, 2014, *available at* http://www.huffingtonpost.com/donald-kerwin/ the-migration-of-unaccomp_b_5512234.html (posting by the Executive Director of the Center for Migration Studies noting that "[a]n unknown, but likely substantial number of migrant children have U.S. resident parents in temporary protected status"). Some have recently suggested that TPS also be granted to these UACs in order to avoid their removal to countries where they face potential domestic or gang violence. *See, e.g.*, Pangea Legal Servs., Re: Provide Temporary Protected Status for Children from El Salvador, Guatemala, Honduras, and Mexico, July 14, 2014 (copy on file with the authors).

[34] INA §274A, 8 U.S.C. §1324a.

[35] INA §274A(h)(3), 8 U.S.C. §1324a(h)(3).

[36] *See generally* 8 U.S.C. §1324a.

[37] When first promulgated in 1987, these regulations were challenged through the administrative process on the grounds that they exceeded the INS's authority. *See* DOJ, INS, Employment Authorization; Classes of Aliens Eligible, 52 Fed. Reg. 46092 (Dec. 4, 1987). Specifically, the challengers asserted that the statutory language referring to aliens "authorized to be ... employed by this chapter or by the Attorney General" did not give the Attorney General authority to grant work authorization "except to those aliens who have already been granted specific authorization by the Act." *Id.* Had this argument prevailed, the authority of the INS and, later, DHS to grant work authorization to beneficiaries of deferred action would have been in doubt, because the INA does not expressly authorize the grant of EADs to such persons. However, the INS rejected this argument on the grounds that the:

> only logical way to interpret this phrase is that Congress, being fully aware of the Attorney General's authority to promulgate regulations, and approving of the manner in which he has exercised that authority in this matter, defined "unauthorized alien" in such fashion as to exclude aliens who have been authorized employment by the Attorney General through the regulatory process, in addition to those who are authorized employment by statute.

Id. Subsequent case law has generally affirmed that immigration officials have broad discretion in determining whether to deny or revoke work authorizations to persons granted deferred action. *See, e.g.*, Perales v. Casillas, 903 F.2d 1043, 1045 (5th Cir. 1990); Chan v. Lothridge, No. 94-16936, 1996 U.S. App. LEXIS 8491 (9th Cir. 1996). These cases also appear to suggest that, by extension, immigration officials have similarly broad discretion to grant work authorization provided any requisite regulatory criteria (e.g., "economic necessity," see, *infra*, note 39) are met.

[38] *See generally* 8 C.F.R. §274a.12.

[39] 8 C.F.R. §274a.12(c)(14). Under these regulations, the "basic criteria" for establishing economic necessity are the federal poverty guidelines. *See* 8 C.F.R. §274a.12(e).

[40] *See generally* CRS Report R43452, *Unlawfully Present Aliens, Driver's Licenses, and Other State-Issued ID: Select Legal Issues*, by Kate M. Manuel and Michael John Garcia; CRS Legal Sidebar WSLG1057, *9th Circuit Decision Enables DACA Beneficiaries—and Other Aliens Granted Deferred Action—to Get Arizona Driver's Licenses*, by Kate M. Manuel.

[41] INA §242(a)(2)(B), 8 U.S.C. §1152(a)(2)(B) (generally barring judicial review of administrative judgments concerning specified forms of discretionary waivers or relief from removal, as well as "any other decision or action of the Attorney General or the Secretary of Homeland Security the authority for which is specified ... [in the INA's immigration] subchapter to be in the discretion of the Attorney General or the Secretary of Homeland Security"). Decisions as to whether to grant an alien asylum, however, may be reviewed to assess whether they are manifestly contrary to the law and constitute an abuse of discretion. *See* INA §242(b)(4)(D), 8 U.S.C. §1152(b)(4)(D).

[42] INA §242(a)(2)(D), 8 U.S.C. §1152(a)(2)(D) (provisions barring review of discretionary actions not precluding "review of constitutional claims or questions of law raised upon a petition for review filed with an appropriate court of appeals"). Most, but not all, reviewing courts have held that this provision permits only the review of "pure" questions of law, and not "mixed" questions involving the application of the law to undisputed facts. *See* Al Ramahi v. Holder, 725 F.3d 1133, 1138 n.2 (9th Cir. 2013) (interpreting the INA to permit judicial review of mixed questions of law and fact, but observing that most other appellate courts have disagreed with this interpretation).

[43] *See, e.g.*, *Congressional Hispanic Caucus Hands DHS Recommendations for Enforcement Changes*, 8 WORKPLACE IMMIGR. REP. 261 (Apr. 14, 2014) (discussing a

memorandum to DHS Secretary Jeh Johnson, which advocated that "extreme hardship" be construed to include family ties to the United States, the age of the qualifying U.S. citizen or LPR relative, and financial and educational hardships, among other things).

[44] The INA also gives immigration officials discretion to waive other statutory requirements. *See, e.g.*, INA §216(c)(4), 8 U.S.C. §1186a(c)(4) (hardship waiver applicable to certain adjustment requirements for conditional permanent resident aliens who are spouses or sons or daughters of U.S. citizens or LPRs); INA §217, 8 U.S.C. §1187 (authorizing establishment of a visa waiver program, under which certain visa requirements may be waived with respect to qualifying aliens from certain countries who seek entry into the United States as tourists for less than 90 days); INA §237(a)(1)(E), 8 U.S.C. §1227(a)(1)(E) (providing for limited waiver of the ground of deportability concerning alien smuggling).

[45] *See* 8 U.S.C. §1182. Aliens who are admitted into the United States as nonimmigrants, or who are paroled into the country, are generally barred from adjusting to LPR status if they are covered by the inadmissibility grounds of INA §245(a), 8 U.S.C. §1255(a).

[46] INA §212(a)(2), 8 U.S.C. §1182(a)(2) (criminal grounds of inadmissibility); INA §212(a)(6)(C), 8 U.S.C. §1182(a)(6)(C) (inadmissibility grounds concerning fraud and misrepresentation).

[47] INA §212(a)(9)(A), 8 U.S.C. §1182(a)(9)(A) (generally providing for a five- or 10-year bar on the admission of an alien who was previously removed, with lengthier or permanent bars applicable in certain circumstances); INA §212(a)(9)(B), 8 U.S.C. §1182(a)(9)(B) (generally establishing either a three- or 10-year bar on the admission of an alien who was unlawfully present in the United States for more than 180 days).

[48] INA §212(d)(3), 8 U.S.C. §1182(d)(3).

[49] INA §245(a), 8 U.S.C. §1255(a).

[50] 8 U.S.C. §1182(a)(9)(B)(v). In 2013, USCIS promulgated regulations which permit unlawfully present alien spouses or children of U.S. citizens who are seeking admission to the United States as legal immigrants to apply for provisional waivers of the bars on admissibility before departing the United States in order to adjust to lawful status. *See generally* CRS Legal Sidebar WSLG385, *Provisional Waivers of the Three- and Ten-Year Bars to Admissibility to Be Granted to Certain Unlawfully Present Aliens*, by Kate M. Manuel.

[51] The use of such a waiver with respect to the drug-related ground of inadmissibility is statutorily limited. Moreover, the commission of certain types of criminal offenses renders an alien ineligible to obtain a waiver. INA §212(h), 8 U.S.C. §1182(h) (barring issuance of waivers to aliens who have committed, or conspired or attempted to commit, murder or acts of torture, and also barring waivers to aliens previously admitted as LPRs who thereafter were convicted of an aggravated felony). *See also* 8 C.F.R. §212.7(e) (providing that waiver authority shall generally not be exercised, "except in extraordinary circumstances," with respect to aliens who seek such a waiver on the basis of hardship caused to U.S. family members but who are inadmissible due to "violent or dangerous crimes"); *Matter of* Jean, 23 I. & N. Dec. 373 (AG 2002) (depending on the gravity of the offense rendering the alien inadmissible, even "exceptional and extremely unusual hardship" likely to be suffered by the alien's U.S. citizen or LPR family members might be inadequate grounds to justify the exercise of waiver authority).

[52] Aliens who are self-petitioners for immigration status under the terms of the Violence Against Women Act (VAWA) are not required to satisfy some of the eligibility requirements to obtain a 212(h) waiver that other classes of aliens must meet. INA §212(h)(1)(C), 8 U.S.C. §1182(h)(1)(C).

[53] INA §212(h), 8 U.S.C. §1182(h) (barring waivers from being issued to former LPRs subsequently convicted of an aggravated felony, or who had not continuously and lawfully resided in the country for at least seven years prior to the initiation of removal proceedings).

[54] INA §212(i), 8 U.S.C. §1182(i) (concerning application of INA §212(a)(6)(C), 8 U.S.C. §1182(a)(6)(C)).

[55] *Id.* Somewhat different eligibility requirements apply to VAWA self-petitioners.

[56] Former INA §212(c), 8 U.S.C. §1182(c) (1994).

[57] *See, e.g.*, Francis v. INS, 532 F.2d 268 (2d Cir. 1976); *Matter of* Silva, 16 I. & N. Dec. 26 (BIA 1976).

[58] *See, e.g.,* Judulang v. Holder,—U.S.—, 132 S. Ct. 476 (2011); INS v. St. Cyr, 533 US 289, 326 (2001) (construing the amendment and subsequent repeal of INA §212(c) in 1996 as not eliminating the availability of waivers for those aliens whose pre-1996 criminal convictions "were obtained through plea agreements and who, notwithstanding those convictions, would have been eligible for § 212(c) relief at the time of their plea under the law then in effect").

[59] Leng May Ma v. Barber, 357 U.S. 185, 189 (1958).

[60] INA §245(a), 8 U.S.C. §1255(a) (potentially enabling parolees to adjust to LPR status, provided that such persons are not covered by any grounds of inadmissibility in INA §212).

[61] *See* 8 C.F.R. §274a.12(a)(4) (authorizing aliens paroled into the United States as refugees to be employed for the period of time they are in that status) & (c)(11) (providing that aliens must apply for work authorization if temporarily paroled into the country "for emergency reasons or reasons deemed strictly in the public interest").

[62] INA §212(d)(5), 8 U.S.C. §1182(d)(5). Prior to the 1980 Refugee Act, which circumscribed the use of parole to facilitate the entry of refugees, parole had regularly been used with respect to persons fleeing persecution. *See* text box, "A Brief History of the Executive Branch's Parole of Aliens into the United States"; 1980 Refugee Act, P.L. 96-212, §202(f) (limiting use of parole for refugees except when there were "compelling reasons in the public interest" to require the alien to be paroled into the country rather than being admitted as a refugee).

[63] Advance parole requests will typically be approved only if certain criteria are met. *See, e.g.*, DHS USCIS, Frequently Asked Questions Concerning Deferred Action for Childhood Arrivals, updated Oct. 23, 2014, *available at* http://www.uscis.gov/humanitarian /consideration-deferred-action-childhood-arrivals-process/frequently-askedquestions (noting that aliens who receive deferred action under the DACA initiative may be able to travel abroad if granted advance parole, and stating that parole will only be granted to enable travel for specific purposes, including a family emergency, or educational or employment purposes).

[64] DHS, USCIS, Parole of Spouses, Children and Parents of Active Duty Members of the U.S. Armed Forces, the Selected Reserve of the Ready Reserve, and Former Members of the U.S. Armed Forces or Selected Reserve of the Ready Reserve and the Effect of Parole on Inadmissibility under Immigration and Nationality Act § 212(a)(6)(A)(i), Nov. 15, 2013 (copy on file with the authors).

[65] Stuart Anderson, National Foundation for American Policy, Executive Action and Legal Immigration, NFAP Policy Brief, at 9 Sept. 2014 (copy on file with the authors) (parole of additional H1-B workers); Marshall Fitz, Center for American Progress, What the President Can Do on Immigration if Congress Fails to Act, at 21-22 (July 2014) (parolein-place of certain family members).

[66] *See* 8 U.S.C. §1182(a)(9)(B)(v).

[67] On the other hand, there could be cases where historical precedent could be said to support particular exercises of discretionary authority, as with the executive branch's practice of continuing to grant DED after the creation of TPS. *See* text box, *supra* page 6.

[68] *See generally* CRS Report R43223, *The Framework for Foreign Workers' Labor Protections Under Federal Law*, by Margaret Mikyung Lee and Jon O. Shimabukuro.

[69] *See generally* DOJ, United States Attorneys' Manual, §9-27.110(B) (2002). There is some debate over the basis for prosecutorial discretion; that is, whether it arises from an English common law procedural mechanism known as the *nolle prosequi*, the structure of the U.S. Constitution, or other sources. *See* "Prosecutorial Discretion Generally," in CRS Report R42924, *Prosecutorial Discretion in Immigration Enforcement: Legal Issues*, by Kate M. Manuel and Todd Garvey.

[70] *See, e.g., Arizona*, 132 S. Ct. at 2498 ("A principal feature of the removal system is the broad discretion entrusted to immigration officials."); Reno v. American-Arab Anti-Discrimination Committee, 525 U.S. 471, 490 (1999) (finding that the various prudential concerns that prompt deference to the executive branch's determinations as to whether to prosecute criminal offenses are "greatly magnified in the deportation context," which involves civil (as opposed to criminal) proceedings). *See also* United States ex rel. Knauff v. Shaughnessy, 338 U.S. 537, 543 (1950) (noting that immigration is a "field where flexibility and the adaptation of the congressional policy to infinitely variable conditions constitute the essence of the program.").

[71] *See, e.g.*, Hanggi v. Holder, 563 F.3d 378, 383 (8th Cir. 2009); Rodrigues v. Attorney General of the United States, 414 Fed. App'x 484, 488 (3d Cir. 2011); *Matter of* Avetisyan, 25 I. & N. Dec. 688 (BIA 2012); *Matter of* Bahta, 22 I. & N. Dec. 1381 (BIA 2000); *Matter of* Singh, 21 I. & N. Dec. 427 (BIA 1996); *Matter of* Ruis, 18 I. & N. Dec. 320 (BIA 1982); *Matter of* Roussis, 18 I. & N. Dec. 256 (BIA 1982); *Matter of* Lennon, 15 I. & N. Dec. 9 (BIA 1974).

[72] *See, e.g., Matter of* G-N-C-, 22 I. & N. Dec. 281 (BIA 1998). *See also* Akhtar v. Gonzales, 450 F.3d 587, 591 (5th Cir. 2006) (recognizing immigration officials' prosecutorial discretion in determining whether to terminate removal proceedings to allow the alien to apply for any immigration benefits that may be available).

[73] *See, e.g., Matter of* Avetisyan, 25 I. & N. Dec. 688 (BIA 2012); *Matter of* York, 22 I. & N. Dec. 660 (BIA 1999); *Matter of* Joseph, 22 I. & N. Dec. 660 (BIA 1990).

[74] *See, e.g.*, DOJ, INS General Counsel Bo Cooper, INS Exercise of Prosecutorial Discretion, July 11, 2000, at 4 (copy on file with the authors) ("The doctrine of prosecutorial discretion applies to enforcement decisions, not benefit decisions. For example, a decision to charge, or not to charge, an alien with a ground of deportability is clearly a prosecutorial enforcement decision. By contrast, the grant of an immigration benefit, such as naturalization or adjustment of status, is a benefit decision that is not a subject for prosecutorial discretion.").

[75] *See, e.g.*, Exercising Prosecutorial Discretion, *supra* note 16 (noting, among the factors to be considered in determining whether a favorable exercise of discretion is warranted, the alien's length of presence in the United States and the circumstances of the alien's arrival in the United States); William J. Howard, Principal Legal Advisor, ICE, DHS, Prosecutorial Discretion, Oct. 24, 2005, at 2 (copy on file with the authors) (similar).

[76] *See, e.g.*, U.S. ICE, Facilitating Parental Interests in the Course of Civil Immigration Enforcement Activities, No. 306-112-002b, Aug. 23, 2013 (copy on file with the authors) ("This and other memoranda related to prosecutorial discretion are designed to ensure that agency resources are focused on our enforcement priorities."); DHS, ICE Director John

Morton, Director, Civil Immigration Enforcement: Priorities for the Apprehension, Detention, and Removal of Aliens, Mar. 2, 2011, at 1-2 (copy on file with the authors) ("ICE ... only has resources to remove approximately 400,000 aliens per year, less than 4 percent of the estimated illegal alien population of the United States."); Prosecutorial Discretion, *supra* note 76 (noting demands created by the establishment of DHS, among other things).

[77] *Cf.* USCIS, Frequently Asked Questions, *supra* note 63 ("Deferred action does not confer lawful [immigration] status upon an individual."). However, individuals granted deferred action are seen as being lawfully present, at least for purposes of federal immigration law, while they have deferred action. *Id.*

[78] *Cf. Reno*, 525 U.S. at 490 ("Postponing justifiable deportation (in the hope that the alien's status will change–by, for example, marriage to an American citizen–or simply with the object of extending the alien's unlawful stay) is often the principal object of resistance to a deportation proceeding.").

[79] *See* sources cited *supra* note 71.

[80] INS, Annual Report of the Immigration and Naturalization Service, at 4 (1962) (copy on file with the authors).

[81] *Id.*

[82] DHS, ICE Director John Morton, *Enforcement Actions at or Focused on Sensitive Locations*, Oct. 24, 2011 (copy on file with the authors).

[83] Civil Immigration Enforcement: Priorities, *supra* note 76, at 1-2.

[84] *See, e.g.*, Congressional Hispanic Caucus Hands DHS Recommendations, *supra* note 43, at 5.

[85] *See* DHS, ICE, *Secure Communities: The Basics*, *available at* http://www.ice.gov/secure_communities (last accessed: Nov. 2, 2014).

[86] *See, e.g.*, Human Rights Watch, *Immigrants "Afraid to Call 911,"* May 15, 2014, *available at* http://www.hrw.org/ news/2014/05/14/us-immigrants-afraid-call-911; Am. Civil Liberties Union, *Domestic Violence Victim's 911 Call for Help Results in Deportation Proceedings*, May 12, 2011, *available at* https://www.aclusocal.org/a-domestic-violencevictims-911-call-for-help-results-in-deportation-proceedings-secure-communities-program-endangers-crime-victims/. In a May 2014 interview on the PBS NewsHour, Secretary of Homeland Security Jeh Johnson said he was taking a "fresh look" at Secure Communities, in part, because of such criticisms. *See* Alex Rogers, *Obama Administration Taking "Fresh Look" at Deportation Review Program*, TIME, May 16, 2014, *available at* http://time.com/102694/obama-deportation-program-reviews/#102694/obama-deportation-program-reviews/.

[87] *See, e.g.*, Hotel & Rest. Employees Union Local 25 v. Smith, 846 F.2d 1499, 1510-1511 (D.C. Cir. 1988); BarahonaGomez v. Reno, 236 F.3d 1115, 1119 n.3 (9th Cir. 2001); Johnson v. INS, 962 F.2d 574, 579 (7th Cir. 1992); Carmona Martinez v. Ashcroft, 118 Fed. App'x 238, 239 (9th Cir. 2004); *Matter of* Yauri, 25 I. & N. Dec. 103 (BIA 2009); *Matter of* Singh, 21 I. & N. Dec. 427 (BIA 1996); *Matter of* Luviano-Rodriguez, 21 I. & N. Dec. 235 (BIA 1996); *Matter of* Quintero, 18 I. & N. Dec. 348 (BIA 1982).

[88] *See* Lennon v. INS, 527 F.2d 187, 191 n.7 (2d Cir. 1975) (describing deferred action as an "informal administrative stay of deportation").

[89] *See generally* Charles Gordon, Stanley Mailman, & Stephen Yale-Loehr, IMMIGR. L. & PROC. §72.03(2)(h) (2009).

[90] By publicizing the availability of deferred action and the criteria applied in determining whether a favorable exercise of discretion is warranted, the DACA initiative could be seen as responding to criticisms that prosecutorial discretion has historically been exercised with little accountability or oversight. *See, e.g.*, Rachel E. Barkow, *Institutional Design and the*

Policing of Prosecutors: Lessons from Administrative Law, 61 STAN. L. REV. 869, 911-916 (2009). In 2007, the USCIS Ombudsman expressly recommended that DHS post information about deferred action on its website, among other things. *See* Recommendation from the CIS Ombudsman to the Director, USCIS, Apr. 6, 2007 (copy on file with the authors).

[91] *Compare* Frequently Asked Questions, *supra* note 63 (grants of deferred action through DACA lasting two years) *with* CHARLES GORDON, STANLEY MAILMAN, & STEPHEN YALE-LOEHR, IMMIGR. L. & PROC. §72.03(2)(h) (2009) (noting "periodic reviews" of non-DACA grants of deferred action to determine whether deferred action is still warranted).

[92] *See, e.g.*, Zachary S. Price, *Enforcement Discretion and Executive Duty*, 67 VAND. L. REV. 671, 675 (2004) (prosecutorial discretion not extending to "entire categories" of aliens); *Dream On*, *supra* note 6, at 846 (similar).

[93] *See* Janet Napolitano, Secretary of Homeland Security, *Exercising Prosecutorial Discretion with Respect to Individuals Who Came to the United States as Children*, June 15, 2012, at 2 (copy on file with the authors) ("[R]equests for relief pursuant to this memorandum are to be decided on a case by case basis.").

[94] *See* Frequently Asked Questions, *supra* note 63 ("[USCIS] retains the ultimate discretion to determine whether deferred action is appropriate in any given case even if the guidelines are met.").

[95] *See, e.g.*, Shoba Sivaprasad Wadhia, *My Great FOIA Adventure and Discoveries of Deferred Action Cases at ICE*, 27 GEO. IMMIGR. L.J. 345, 350 (2013) (reporting that ICE processed 698 deferred action cases in the first three quarters of FY2012). By contrast, USCIS reports that it granted 1,707 requests for deferred action through DACA in September 2012 alone. *See* USCIS, *Deferred Action for Childhood Arrivals Process* (Nov. 2012 reporting date), *available at* http://www.uscis.gov/sites/default/files/USCIS/Resources/Reports%20and%20 Studies/ Immigration%20Forms%20Data/Static_files/2012-1116%20DACA%20Monthly% 20Report.pdf.

[96] *See, e.g.*, Randy Capps & Marc R. Rosenblum, Executive Action for Unauthorized Immigrants, Migration Policy Institute Issue Brief No. 10, at 3 (Sept. 2014) (discussing how many aliens might be affected if deferred action were granted to certain segments of the population of unlawfully present aliens).

[97] For a discussion of standing, see the text box, "Who Has Standing to Challenge Exercises of Enforcement Discretion?", *infra* page 20.

[98] *Heckler*, 470 U.S. 832-833 n.4 (internal citations omitted).

[99] The *Heckler* Court cited the U.S. Court of Appeals for the District of Columbia Circuit's decision in *Adams v. Richardson* in support of its view that a policy of nonenforcement could constitute abdication, but does not otherwise attempt to define the parameters of what could be said to be abdication.

[100] Texas v. United States, 106 F.3d 661, 667 (5th Cir. 1997).

[101] *Id.*

[102] *See, e.g.*, Lopez v. Davis, 531 U.S. 230, 241 (2001) ("Congress' use of the permissive 'may' in §3621(e)(2)(B) contrasts with the legislators' use of a mandatory 'shall' in the very same section. Elsewhere in §3621, Congress used 'shall' to impose discretionless obligations, including the obligation to provide drug treatment when funds are available. *See* 18 U.S.C. §3621(e)(1) ('Bureau of Prisons shall, subject to the availability of appropriations, provide residential substance abuse treatment (and make arrangements for appropriate aftercare)'); *see also, e.g.*, §3621(b) ('The Bureau shall designate the place of the prisoner's

imprisonment.... In designating the place of imprisonment or making transfers under this subsection, there shall be no favoritism given to prisoners of high social or economic status.'").

[103] Crane v. Napolitano, No. 3:12-cv-03247-O, 2013 U.S. Dist. LEXIS 57788, *27-*39 (N.D. Tex., Apr. 23, 2013).

[104] *See* INA §235(a)(1), (a)(3), & (b)(2)(A), 8 U.S.C. §1225(a)(1), (a)(3), & (b)(2)(A).

[105] *Crane*, No. 3:12-cv-03247-O, Order (N.D. Tex., July 31, 2013) (copy on file with the authors).

[106] Moreover, even if the district court's interpretation were adopted, an argument could be made that the provisions of the INA discussed by the district court require only that arriving aliens be placed in removal proceedings, not that removal proceedings be pursued to a decision on the merits or, if the alien is found removal, until he or she is removed.

[107] The statute at issue in *Heckler*, for example, stated that "[a]ny article of food, drug, or cosmetic that is adulterated or misbranded when introduced into or while in interstate commerce or while held for sale ... after shipment in interstate commerce, or which may not ... be introduced into interstate commerce, *shall be liable to be proceeded against*." 470 U.S. at 835 (quoting 21 U.S.C. §334(a)(1) (emphasis added)). Nonetheless, despite its use of "shall," this statutory provision was seen by the Court as "framed in the permissive." *Id.*

[108] *Matter of* E-R-M & L-R-M, 25 I. & N. Dec. 520, 523 (BIA 2011).

[109] *Id.* at 522.

[110] 467 U.S. 837, 842-43 (1984).

[111] *Id.* at 843.

[112] *See, e.g.*, Morton v. Ruiz, 415 U.S. 199, 231 (1974) ("The power of an administrative agency to administer a congressionally created and funded program necessarily requires the formulation of policy and the making of rules to fill any gap left, implicitly or explicitly, by Congress.").

[113] *See, e.g.*, Christensen v. Harris County, 529 U.S. 576, 587 (2000) ("Interpretations such as those in opinion letters - like interpretations contained in policy statements, agency manuals, and enforcement guidelines, all of which lack the force of law - do not warrant *Chevron*-style deference."). Instead, such "informal" interpretations may be afforded a lesser degree of deference that depends upon various factors including "the degree of the agency's care, its consistency, formality, and relative expertness, and ... the persuasiveness of the agency's position," as well as the "writer's thoroughness, logic, and expertise, its fit with prior interpretations, and any other source of weight." United States v. Mead Corp., 533 U.S. 218, 228, 235 (2001); *see also* Skidmore v. Swift, 323 U.S. 134 (1944).

[114] *See supra* note 43.

[115] Executive Action and Legal Immigration, *supra* note 65; Gary Endelman & Cyrus D. Mehta, The Family That Is Counted Together Stays Together: How to Eliminate Immigrant Visa Backlogs, Sept. 15, 2014, *available at* http://blog.cyrusmehta.com/2014/09/the-family-that-is-counted-together.html; American Immigration Lawyers Ass'n, Letter to Cecilia Muñoz, Assistant to the President and Director of the Domestic Policy Council, Aug. 6, 2014, at 2 (copy on file with the authors).

[116] *See* INA §203(d), 8 U.S.C. §1153(d) (providing that derivatives are entitled to the "same status, and the same order of consideration," as the principals they accompany (or follow to join) in immigrating).

[117] 8 U.S.C. §1153(d).

[118] Executive Action and Legal Immigration, *supra*, note 65, at 3.

[119] *See* sources cited, *supra* note 115.

[120] In particular, under INA §201(b), 8 U.S.C. §1151(b), immediate relatives of U.S. citizens, special immigrants, or aliens granted cancellation of removal are expressly exempted from being counted against the annual limits on the number of immigrants admitted, but derivatives of immigrants admitted on employment- or family-based visas are not. Because Congress clearly identified parties who should not be counted, an argument could be made that the statute precludes the Executive from using its discretion not to count derivatives, as Congress did not list them among the persons exempted from counting.

[121] *See, e.g.*, Letter to Cecilia Muñoz, *supra* note 115, at 3.

[122] INA §245(a), 8 U.S.C. §1255(a).

[123] *See, e.g.*, Flores v. USCIS, 718 F.3d 548 (6th Cir. 2013) ("USCIS argues that Mr. Suazo and other TPS beneficiaries who initially entered the United States without inspection and have an independent basis for a visa can never satisfy the threshold requirement of being 'admitted or paroled' or 'admissible.' The USCIS argues that Suazo is only allowed protection under TPS as long as the designation is conferred upon him. USCIS argues that he is unable to adjust to LPR under the independent basis—through his wife's application—because he was not admitted."); Denise A. Vanison, Policy and Strategy, USCIS, et al., Memorandum to Alejandro N. Mayorkas, *Administrative Alternatives to Comprehensive Immigration Reform*, undated (copy on file with the authors) ("Individuals in TPS continue to be deemed ineligible to adjust or change status in the U.S. based on legal opinions rendered in the early 1990s by a General Counsel of the former Immigration and Naturalization Service (INS).").

[124] Alternatives to Comprehensive Immigration Reform, *supra* note 123, at 1.

[125] *See, e.g.*, Letter to Cecilia Muñoz, *supra* note 115, at 3.

[126] *See Flores*, 718 F.3d at 553.

[127] *See supra* note 110 and accompanying text.

[128] *See supra* note 111 and accompanying text.

[129] 545 U.S. 967, 981 (2009).

[130] *Id.*; *see also* Motor Vehicle Manufacturers Ass'n v. State Farm Ins., 463 U.S. 29 (1983).

[131] *See, e.g.*, Mortgage Bankers Ass'n v. Harris, 720 F.3d 966 (D.C. Cir. 2013); Alaska Professional Hunters Ass'n v. FAA, 177 F.3d 1030 (D.C. Cir. 1999).

[132] Miller v. California Speedway Corp., 536 F.3d 1020 (9th Cir. 2008), *cert. denied*, 555 U.S. 1208 (2009); Warder v. Shalala, 149 F.3d 73, 75-79 (1st Cir. 1998), *cert. denied*, 526 U.S. 1064 (1999).

[133] *See Perez v. Mortgage Bankers Association & Nickols v. Mortgage Bankers Association*, 134 S. Ct. 2820 (2014).

[134] 529 U.S. 120, 133 (2000).

[135] *Id.* at 159. *See also id.* at 133 ("In addition, we must be guided to a degree by common sense as to the manner in which Congress is likely to delegate a policy decision of such economic and political magnitude to an administrative agency."). *See also MCI v. AT&T*, 512 U.S. 218 (1994) (rejecting the Federal Communications Commission's (FCC's) interpretation of a statutory provision permitting it to "modify" requirements under a specific provision of its governing act to eliminate a tariff requirement on the grounds that de-tariffing was a "major" and "fundamental" change, which would eliminate a "crucial provision of the statute for 40% of a major sector of the industry" regulated by the FCC).

[136] *See, e.g.*, Abigail R. Moncrieff, Reincarnating the "Major Questions" Exception to *Chevron* Deference as a Doctrine of Non-Interference (Or Why Massachusetts v. EPA Got It Wrong), Harvard Law School Faculty Scholarship Series Paper 12 (2008), at 1 (copy on file with the authors). At least one commentator has taken issue with the view that this

exception forecloses recent Obama Administration actions. *See* Dan Farber, Is It Unconstitutional for the President to Implement Major New Policies by Regulation?, Feb. 3, 2014, *available at* http://blogs.berkeley.edu/2014/02/03/is-itunconstitutional-for-the-president-to-implement-major-new-policies-by-regulation/.

In: Presidential Executive Action on Immigration ISBN: 978-1-63482-263-3
Editor: David Ferguson

Chapter 2

THE OBAMA ADMINISTRATION'S NOVEMBER 2014 IMMIGRATION INITIATIVES: QUESTIONS AND ANSWERS*

Kate M. Manuel

SUMMARY

On November 20, 2014, President Obama delivered a televised address wherein he broadly described the steps that his administration is taking to "fix" what he has repeatedly described as a "broken immigration system." Following the President's address, executive agencies made available intra-agency memoranda and fact sheets detailing specific actions that have already been taken, or will be taken in the future. These actions generally involve either border security, the current unlawfully present population, or future legal immigration.

The most notable of these actions, for many commentators, are the initiatives to grant "deferred action"—one type of relief from removal—to some unlawfully present aliens who were brought to the United States as children and raised here, or who have children who are U.S. citizens or lawfully permanent resident (LPR) aliens. Previously, in June 2012, then Secretary of Homeland Security Janet Napolitano announced a program—commonly known as Deferred Action for Childhood Arrivals

---

* This is an edited, reformatted and augmented version of a Congressional Research Service publication R43798, prepared for Members and Committees of Congress, dated November 24, 2014.

(DACA)—whereby unlawfully present aliens who had been brought to the United States as children and met other criteria could receive deferred action and, in many cases, employment authorization. The eligibility criteria for DACA expressly excluded unlawfully present aliens who were over 31 years of age, or who had entered the United States on or after June 15, 2007. However, aliens who are over 31 years of age, or entered between June 15, 2007, and January 1, 2010, could receive deferred action as part of the 2014 initiative.

Similarly, unlawfully present aliens who have children who are U.S. citizens or LPRs could also receive deferred action and employment authorization pursuant to the November 2014 initiatives, provided they meet specified criteria. These criteria include "continuous residence" in the United States since before January 1, 2010; physical presence in the United States both on the date the initiative was announced and on the date when they request deferred action; and not being an enforcement priority (e.g., not a threat to national or border security).

The announced executive actions—particularly the granting of deferred action and employment authorization to unlawfully present aliens—have revived debate about the President's discretionary authority over immigration like that which followed the announcement of DACA in 2012. In the case of DACA, some argued that the initiative violates the Take Care Clause of the U.S. Constitution, runs afoul of specific requirements found in the Immigration and Nationality Act (INA), or is inconsistent with historical precedents. Others, however, asserted that DACA involves a valid exercise of the executive's prosecutorial or enforcement discretion, is consistent with the INA, and has ample historical precedent. Similar arguments will likely be made as to the November 2014 actions, which affect a significantly larger number of aliens than DACA.

Legal challenges to DACA have generally failed on standing grounds, because the plaintiffs bringing these challenges were not seen as the proper parties to seek judicial relief from a federal court. The one exception to this—the litigation in *Crane v. Napolitano*—resulted in the reviewing federal district court finding that DACA runs afoul of provisions in Section 235 of the INA which some assert require the executive to place unlawfully present aliens in removal proceedings. However, this same federal district court subsequently found that it lacked jurisdiction because the plaintiff immigration officers alleged that they faced discipline by their employer, DHS, if they refused to implement DACA, and such claims are within the jurisdiction of the Merit Systems Protection Board (MSPB), not the court.

The 113th Congress has also considered legislation to defund DACA (e.g., H.R. 5272, H.R. 5316).

On November 20, 2014, President Obama delivered a televised address wherein he broadly described the steps that his administration is taking to "fix" what he has repeatedly described as a "broken immigration system."[1] Following the President's address, executive agencies made available intra-agency memoranda and fact sheets detailing specific actions that have already been taken, or will be taken in the future.[2] These actions generally involve either border security, the current unlawfully present population, or future legal immigration.

The announced executive actions—particularly the granting of deferred action and employment authorization to some unlawfully present aliens, discussed below (see "Unlawfully Present Population")—have revived debate about the executive's discretionary authority over immigration like that which followed the Administration's June 2012 announcement of the Deferred Action for Childhood Arrivals (DACA) initiative.[3] DACA has permitted some unlawfully present aliens who were brought to the United States as children and raised here to obtain temporary relief from removal and, in many cases, employment authorization. Some have argued that DACA constitutes an abdication of the executive's duty to enforce the laws and runs afoul of specific requirements found in the Immigration and Nationality Act (INA),[4] among other things. Others, however, have maintained that the DACA initiative is a lawful exercise of the discretionary authority conferred on the executive by the Constitution and federal statute.[5] Similar arguments will likely be made as to the November 2014 actions, which affect a significantly larger number of aliens than DACA.

This report provides the answers to key legal questions related to the various immigration-related actions announced by the Obama Administration on November 20, 2014. Because the various documents outlining these actions have been available for a limited period of time, and additional information is expected to be released in the future, these answers are necessarily preliminary.

What Actions Are Being Taken by the Obama Administration?

Following the President's televised speech, executive branch agencies and, in two cases, the White House announced dozens of specific actions as to immigration. These actions can be broadly divided into the same three categories noted by the President in his speech: (1) border security, (2) the current unlawfully present population, and (3) future legal immigration.

Border Security

Among the Administration's actions is "implement[ing] a Southern Border and Approaches Campaign Strategy to fundamentally alter the way in which we marshal resources to the border."[6] This will involve the Department of Homeland Security (DHS) commissioning three task forces made up of various law enforcement agencies. These task forces will focus on the southern maritime border, the southern land border and West Coast, and investigations to support the other two task forces. Among the objectives of the new strategy are increasing the perceived risk of engaging in or facilitating "illegal transnational or cross-border activity" (a term which could include the migration of persons); interdicting people who attempt to enter illegally between ports of entry; and preventing the "illegal exploitation of legal flows" (which could include things such as alien smuggling at ports of entry).[7]

Unlawfully Present Population

The Administration also proposes several actions affecting the current population of unlawfully present aliens, which is widely estimated to include some 11 million persons.[8] Arguably the most notable of these actions are the initiatives to grant deferred action—one type of relief from removal—to some unlawfully present aliens who were brought to the United States as children and raised here, or who have children who are U.S. citizens or lawfully permanent resident (LPR) aliens.[9] Previously, in June 2012, then-Secretary of Homeland Security Janet Napolitano announced a program—commonly known as Deferred Action for Childhood Arrivals (DACA)— whereby unlawfully present aliens who had been brought to the United States as children and met other criteria could receive deferred action and, in many cases, employment authorization.[10] The eligibility criteria for DACA expressly excluded unlawfully present aliens who were over 31 years of age, or who had entered the United States on or after June 15, 2007.[11] However, aliens who are over 31 years of age, or entered the United States between June 15, 2007, and January 1, 2010, could receive deferred action as part of the November 2014 initiative.[12] The 2014 initiative would also extend the duration of grants of deferred action (and work authorization) received by DACA beneficiaries from the current two years, to three years.[13]

In addition, unlawfully present aliens who have children who are U.S. citizens or LPRs will also be eligible for deferred action (and employment authorization) pursuant to the November 2014 initiatives, provided they meet specified criteria.[14] These criteria include (1) "continuous residence" in the United States since before January 1, 2010; (2) physical presence in the United

States both on the date the initiative was announced (i.e., November 20, 2014) and when they request deferred action; (3) not being an enforcement priority under the Administration's newly announced priorities, discussed below; and (4) "present[ing] no other factors that, in the exercise of discretion, makes the grant of deferred action inappropriate."[15]

Aliens granted deferred action pursuant to these initiatives—or otherwise[16]—are eligible for employment authorization upon showing "an economic necessity for employment."[17]

Other notable actions as to the current population of unlawfully present aliens include

- revising DHS's priorities for civil immigration enforcement by, among other things, narrowing the scope of aliens who are considered "highest priority" for removal.[18] Under the revised priorities, aliens without legal immigration status who have been in the United States since 2013, and who have not engaged in specified criminal activity or violated a prior order of removal, seem unlikely to be considered a removal priority.
- ending the Secure Communities program and replacing it with another program, known as the Priority Enforcement Program (PEP).[19] PEP will resemble Secure Communities in that Secure Communities also utilized information sharing between various levels and agencies of government to identify potentially removable aliens.[20] However, unlike Secure Communities, PEP will focus on aliens who have been convicted of felonies or "significant" misdemeanors, and generally will not entail states and localities holding aliens after they would have otherwise been released for the state or local offense that prompted their initial arrest so that DHS can take custody of them.[21]
- ensuring uniform recognition of grants of "advance parole" by immigration agencies, so that aliens without legal status who depart the United States for another country pursuant to a grant of advance parole are not excluded from the United States upon their return on the grounds that they "departed" the United States and, thus, triggered the 3- and 10-year bars upon the admission of aliens who have accrued more than 180 days of unlawful presence in the United States, discussed below.[22] (Parole is a device which permits an alien to enter the United States without satisfying the criteria for admissibility set forth in INA §212(a). With advance parole, an alien without legal status who is present in the United States is effectively granted a

limited assurance, prior to departing the United States for another country, that s/he will be permitted to re-enter the United States upon his/her return.)

- granting "parole in place" or deferred action to some immediate relatives of U.S. citizens and LPRs who "seek to enlist in the Armed Forces," instead of just to qualifying relatives of active Armed Service personnel, the standing Reserves, or veterans of the Armed Services or standing Reserves.[23] (While parole is typically granted to aliens outside the United States who are ineligible for admission under INA §212(a), parole in place entails granting parole to unlawfully present aliens within the United States.)[24]

Legal Immigration

In addition, the Obama Administration announced several actions which it characterizes as "support[ing] our county's high-skilled businesses and workers."[25] Included among these actions are as yet-to-be-determined steps to ensure that all immigrant visas authorized by Congress for issuance in a particular year are issued (assuming demand).[26] Previously, delays in processing applications for immigrant visas resulted in some visas going unused (less than 5% of all available immigrant visas in recent years).[27] This, in turn, prompted calls for Congress or the executive to "recapture" unused visas (i.e., to identify unused visa numbers from earlier years and make them available for current use).[28] The Obama Administration's November 20, 2014, action does not purport to recapture previously unused visas. However, it can be seen as an attempt to avoid the perceived need for visa recapture in the future by ensuring that all immigrant visas available for issuance in a year are used. Relatedly, the Administration proposes as-yetunspecified steps to "improve the system for determining when immigrant visas are available to applicants during the fiscal year," as well as consideration of "other regulatory or policy changes" to "better assist and provide stability" to be beneficiaries of employment-based immigrant visa petitions, including by ensuring that visa petitions remain valid when the alien beneficiary of the petition seeks to change employers or jobs.[29]

Another action involves expanding the duration of any "optional practical training" (OPT) engaged in by foreign nationals studying science, technology, engineering, and mathematics (STEM) fields at institutions of higher education in the United States on non-immigrant F-1 student visas, as well as "expand[ing] the degree programs" eligible for OPT.[30] Foreign nationals studying in the United States on F-1 visas have long been able to request an additional 12 months of F-1 visa status for temporary employment—known as OPT—in their field of study.[31] Regulations promulgated in 2008 permitted students in STEM fields to request an additional 17 months of OPT, for a total of 29 months of OPT.[32] However, only students in STEM fields are eligible for this 17 month extension, and these students can participate in OPT for no more than 29 months. Because any expansion of OPT can be seen, at least by some, as affecting employment opportunities for U.S. persons,[33] the Administration also proposes to "improve" the OPT program by requiring "stronger ties" to degree-granting institutions, and "tak[ing] steps" to ensure that OPT employment is consistent with U.S. labor market protections.[34]

Other actions announced by the Obama Administration include

- making greater use of provisions in INA §203(b)(2)(B), which permit aliens with advanced degrees or "exceptional ability" to obtain an immigrant visa without a sponsoring employer—as is generally required for immigrants who are not sponsored by family members—if their admission is in the "national interest."
- using the authority granted to the Executive in INA §212(d)(5)(A) to "parole" aliens into the United States when there is a "significant public benefit" to permit some inventors, researchers, and founders of start-up enterprises to enter and lawfully remain in the United States without a visa (or counting against the visa caps).[35]
- clarifying and standardizing the meaning of "specialized knowledge" for purposes of the L-1B visa program, which allows companies to transfer certain employees who are executives or managers, or have "specialized knowledge" of the company or its processes, to the United States from the company's foreign operations.
- clarifying what is meant by the "same or similar job" for purposes of INA §204(j), which provides that employment-based immigrant visa petitions remain valid when the alien employee changes jobs or employers so long as the new job is in the "same or similar occupational classification" as the job for which the petition was filed.
- reviewing the so-called PERM program, whereby the Department of Labor (DOL) certifies that the issuance of an employment-based immigrant visa will not displace U.S. workers, or adversely affect the wages or working conditions of similarly employed U.S. workers, to identify methods for aligning domestic worker recruitment requirements with demonstrated occupational shortages and surpluses.

- DOL "certifying"[36] applications for nonimmigrant T visas for aliens who have been victims of human trafficking, as well as certifying applications for nonimmigrant U visas for eligible victims of extortion, forced labor, and fraud in foreign labor contracting that DOL detects in the course of its workplace investigations.
- establishing an interagency working group to "streamline" the immigrant visa system, in part, by improving services and reducing employers' burdens.[37]

Other

Other announced actions do not neatly fall into any of the foregoing categories or, in one case, could be said to involve multiple categories. Arguably key among these is the expansion of a preexisting Obama Administration program that provides for "provisional waivers" of the 3- and 10-year bars on the admission of aliens who have accrued more than 180 days of unlawful presence in the United States. Initially, this program reached only spouses, sons, or daughters of U.S. citizens. It will now be expanded to include qualifying relatives of LPRs.[38]

As a general matter, unlawfully present aliens whose spouses or parents are U.S. citizens or LPRs may be eligible for an immigrant visa and adjustment to legal status. Obtaining such an immigrant visa typically requires the alien to leave the United States so that his/her visa application can be processed by U.S. consular officers overseas.[39] However, leaving the country generally triggers the application of the 3- and 10-year bars if the alien has been unlawfully present in the United States for more than 180 days (as most unlawfully present aliens have been).[40] These bars can be waived if denial of the alien's admission would result in "extreme hardship" to the alien's spouse or parents.[41] However, the time required to obtain a waiver after leaving the country and triggering the bar has historically kept many unlawfully present aliens who could "legalize their status" under current law (see "Does granting deferred action to unlawfully present aliens legalize their status?") from doing so. In 2013, the Obama Administration began allowing spouses or children of U.S. citizens to request and obtain provisional waivers of the 3- and 10-year bars to their admission while they are in the United States (they generally still must travel outside the United States for processing).[42] However, the spouses and children of LPRs were ineligible for such provisional waivers until the 2014 actions.

Other actions announced in November 2014 include certain personnel reforms involving immigration and customs officers;[43] promoting naturalization by eligible LPRs;[44] establishing an interagency task force on "New Americans" to "increase meaningful engagement" between immigrants and the communities where they settle;[45] and establishing an interagency working group to address the interplay of immigration and employment law.[46]

Did the President Issue an Executive Order?

As of November 24, 2014, the President has not issued an executive order regarding these immigration-related actions; nor has he given any indication that he will issue such an order. With the exception of several specific actions announced in two presidential memoranda,[47] all other actions to date—including the granting of deferred action to some unlawfully present aliens—have been announced in intra-agency memoranda or fact sheets made available by executive agencies after the President's televised address. This is arguably consistent with prior actions in the field of immigration and, particularly, prior exercises of discretion in enforcing federal immigration law. For example, the 1990 "Family Fairness" program, discussed below—which gave certain unlawfully present aliens temporary relief from deportation (later known as removal)—was announced in a memorandum from the head of the Immigration and Naturalization Service (INS) to regional officials.[48] Similarly, President Clinton relied on a memorandum to the Attorney General when authorizing deferred enforced departure (DED)— another type of temporary relief from removal—for some unlawfully present aliens from Liberia.[49]

The fact that these actions were announced by means other than an executive order generally would not affect their permissibility. In other words, whether the deferred action initiatives, for example, are permissible depends upon whether the executive has the legal authority to grant this relief, not whether the initiatives were announced by means of an executive order or a memorandum from the Secretary of Homeland Security.

What Is the Legal Authority for the Administration's Actions?

Although each specific Administration action involves somewhat different legal authorities, three broad types of legal authority can be said to underlie all these actions: (1) prosecutorial or enforcement discretion; (2) express delegations of authority to the executive by Congress; and (3) the executive's discretion in interpreting and applying immigration law when congressional enactments are "silent or ambiguous" on specific issues.

Prosecutorial or Enforcement Discretion

The judicial and executive branches have repeatedly recognized that the determination as to whether to grant deferred action to an individual alien is a matter of prosecutorial or enforcement discretion.[50] Such discretion has generally been seen as an independent attribute of the executive branch, and does not arise from—or require—an express delegation of authority by Congress.[51] Thus, the fact that Congress has not authorized the executive to grant deferred action to aliens in the circumstances contemplated here (i.e., unlawfully present aliens brought to the United States as children or whose children are U.S. citizens or LPRs) does not, in itself, make such a grant impermissible.[52]

Prosecutorial discretion is generally seen as affording the executive wide latitude in determining when, against whom, how, and even whether to prosecute apparent violations of federal law.[53] However, the Constitution or federal statutes could potentially impose certain constraints upon this discretion, as discussed below (see "Are there constitutional or related constraints upon the executive's discretionary authority over immigration enforcement?" and "What other legal issues might be raised by the Administration's actions?").

Express Delegations of Statutory Authority

In other cases, Congress has expressly granted certain authority to the executive that the Obama Administration would appear to rely upon for specific actions. For example, the definition of *unauthorized alien* in INA §274A(h)(3) has historically been seen to give the executive the authority to grant employment authorization documents (EADs) to aliens who are not expressly authorized to work by the INA. Section 274A(h)(3)'s definition describes an unauthorized alien as an alien who is not "authorized to be ... employed ... by the Attorney General [currently, the Secretary of Homeland Security]."[54] The immigration agencies have relied upon this definition in promulgating regulations that permit aliens granted deferred action to receive EADs upon showing "an economic necessity for employment."[55]

Other actions that would appear to involve express delegations of statutory authority include (but are not limited to) (1) paroling into the United States some inventors, researchers, and founders of start-up enterprises on public interest grounds (INA §212(d)(5));[56] (2) granting provisional waivers of the 3-

and 10-year bars upon the admissibility of aliens who have accrued more than 180 days of unlawful presence in the United States (INA §212(a)(9)(B)(v)); and (3) permitting aliens with advanced degrees or "exceptional ability" to obtain an immigrant visa without a sponsoring employer if their admission is in the "national interest" (INA §203(b)(2)(B)).

Any exercise of delegated authority must be consistent with the terms of the delegation, as discussed below (see "What other legal issues might be raised by the Administration's actions?"). Questions could also be raised about whether particular exercises of authority are consistent with historical practice, other provisions of the INA, or congressional intent.[57]

Executive Discretion When Statutes Are "Silent or Ambiguous"

In yet other cases, the Obama Administration would appear to be relying upon the deference generally given to the executive in interpreting and applying statutes in taking certain actions. As the Supreme Court articulated in its 1984 decision in *Chevron U.S.A. v. Natural Resources Defense Council,* when "Congress has directly spoken to the issue, ... that is the end of the matter; for the court, as well as the agency, must give effect to the unambiguously expressed intent of Congress."[58] However, where a statute is "silent or ambiguous with respect to a specific issue," courts will generally defer to an agency interpretation that is based on a "permissible construction of the statute,"[59] on the grounds that the executive branch must fill any "gaps" explicitly or implicitly left by Congress in the course of administering congressional programs.[60]

Among the gaps that Congress could be said to have left in the INA for the executive to fill are (1) what constitutes "extreme hardship" for purposes of the 3- and 10-year bars upon the admission of aliens who have accrued more than 180 days of unlawful presence in the United States; (2) the duration of any OPT for F-1 student visas holders; (3) what steps are to be taken to ensure that all immigrant visas available for issuance in a given year are used; and (4) what constitutes "specialized knowledge" for purposes of the L-1B visa program. The Obama Administration's November 20, 2014, actions can be seen to address all of these "gaps," as well as others not specifically noted here.

Any construction advanced by the executive must, however, constitute a "permissible" and "reasonable" interpretation of the underlying statute in order to be afforded deference by the courts, as previously noted. Also, the executive has no discretion in interpreting or applying the law where Congress has spoken to the precise question at issue.[61]

Are There Constitutional or Related Constraints upon the Executive's Discretionary Authority over Immigration Enforcement?[62]

The Constitution confers upon the President the responsibility and obligation to "take Care that the Law is faithfully executed."[63] Some of the Obama Administration's immigration actions— including the identification of particular categories of aliens as priorities for removal, and the expanded use of deferred action to afford certain unlawfully present aliens with temporary relief from removal—are primarily premised upon executive assertions of independent constitutional authority.[64] As previously noted, the executive branch is understood to have substantial discretionary authority to determine when and whether to pursue sanctions against apparent violators of federal law, an authority generally referred to as prosecutorial or enforcement discretion.[65] Prosecutorial discretion is most closely associated with executive enforcement of federal criminal law.[66] But the concept of prosecutorial or enforcement discretion is often applicable in civil contexts as well, including with respect to immigration officers' decisions regarding whether to seek the removal of aliens who have entered or remained in the United States in violation of federal immigration law. [67]

A decision not to pursue sanctions against a particular individual is generally understood to be largely shielded from judicial review.[68] Nonetheless, there are recognized limitations to the scope of this discretionary authority.[69] As an initial matter, a general enforcement policy that is promulgated by an agency may not enjoy the same degree of immunity from judicial review as individual determinations not to pursue sanctions in a particular case.[70] Moreover, courts have recognized that agency action must be consistent with congressional objectives underlying the statutory scheme it administers. When adopting a general enforcement policy, an agency may not rely on factors "which Congress has not intended it to consider"[71] and substitute its own policy judgment for that which has been made by Congress. In particular, a general policy of non-enforcement by an agency could potentially be reviewable by a court and found to be an impermissible "abdication" of the agency's statutory responsibilities.[72]

Whether the Obama Administration's November deferred action initiatives constitute a permissible exercise of enforcement discretion will be the subject of heated debate. This debate will likely center upon the Administration's identification of large numbers of unlawfully present aliens as non-priorities for removal, as well as the expansion of its earlier deferred action initiative to additional aliens.[73] On one hand, it could be argued that aspects of these initiatives functionally constitute a blanket policy of non-enforcement of federal immigration statutes, and that this non-enforcement policy represents an abdication of DHS's statutory responsibilities to enforce federal immigration law.[74] The INA contains several grounds of removal which are potentially applicable to aliens who may receive deferred action under the Administration's initiative.[75] Moreover, while federal statute grants immigration authorities the power to provide some unlawfully present aliens with relief from removal, these statute-based forms of relief are limited in scope.[76] It could be argued that the Administration's decision to focus enforcement resources almost exclusively on certain categories of removable aliens, while declining to pursue the removal of a substantial portion of the unauthorized population which does not fall within those categories, constitutes an abdication of its responsibilities under the INA. It might also be argued that, by enabling a sizeable portion of the unlawfully present population to request deferred action (a form of relief that is not expressly authorized by federal statute, except in narrow circumstances[77]) and work authorization, the executive branch is impermissibly substituting its own judgment as to whom should be legally allowed to remain in the United States for that of Congress.

On the other hand, it could be argued that resource constraints preclude DHS from pursuing the removal of all unlawfully present aliens in the United States,[78] and that the decision to focus resources primarily upon the removal of those who have engaged in criminal activity, pose a threat to public safety, or recently entered the United States is consistent with applicable statutory enactments.[79]Additionally, while the Administration's initiative would grant some unlawfully present aliens legal permission to remain in the United States for a specified period, it would not provide them with legal immigration status, or enable them to acquire benefits they are statutorily barred from receiving.[80] The executive might further dispute arguments that the initiative constitutes a blanket policy of non-enforcement, and note that immigration officers retain ultimate discretion to grant deferred action on a case-by case basis, and that they are not barred from seeking the removal of unlawfully present aliens who have not been identified by DHS as enforcement priorities.[81] It might also be argued that, particularly in light of the long-standing executive practice of granting deferred action and other forms of relief from removal, that Congress has implicitly signaled its approval or acquiescence to the executive's use of these forms of administrative relief, and the INA should not be interpreted to preclude the executive from granting such relief in certain instances.[82]

Accordingly, it could be argued that the executive branch's action, while affecting a substantial number of unlawfully present aliens, does not constitute a legally impermissible abdication of its statutory duties.

What Other Legal Issues Might Be Raised by the Administration's Actions?

In some cases, specific actions taken by the Obama Administration could potentially be seen to run afoul of the provisions of the INA, in which case the executive action could be found to be impermissible (provided a plaintiff with standing to challenge the executive action were found (see "Who has standing to challenge the Administration's initiatives?")).[83] For example, one federal district court recently found that DACA is contrary to three purportedly "interlocking provisions" in INA §235 which some assert require that unlawfully present aliens be placed in removal proceedings.[84] These provisions state that

- any alien present in the United States who has not been admitted *shall* be deemed an applicant for admission;
- applicants for admission *shall* be inspected by immigration officers; and
- in the case of an alien who is an applicant for admission, if the examining immigration officer determines that an alien seeking admission is not clearly and beyond a doubt entitled to be admitted, the alien *shall* be detained for removal proceedings.[85]

Thus, the district court concluded that DACA runs afoul of the INA because many of the aliens granted deferred action through DACA had never been placed in removal proceedings as required, in the court's view, by INA §235. (This same court, however, later ruled that it lacked jurisdiction over the case.[86] That decision has been appealed, and it is presently unclear whether and how the court's earlier decision construing INA §235 could be seen to restrain any future grants of deferred action.[87])

Similar statutory constraints could potentially be also be implicated in other Obama Administration actions, particularly as executive agencies take action to clarify the meaning and application of certain statutory language. For example, INA §212(a)(9)(B)(v) would appear to preclude DHS—in issuing guidance regarding waivers of the 3- and 10-year bars upon the admission of aliens who have been unlawfully present in the United States for more than 180 days—from granting waivers based on mere "hardship," as opposed to "extreme hardship," or from considering hardship to U.S. citizen or LPR children, as opposed to U.S. citizen or LPR spouses or parents. This is because INA §212(a)(9)(B)(v) expressly refers to waivers

> in the case of an immigrant who is the *spouse or son or daughter of a United States citizen or of an alien lawfully admitted for permanent residence*, if it is established ... that the refusal of admission to such [an] alien would result in extreme hardship to the *citizen or lawfully resident spouse or parent* of such alien.[88]

Does Granting Deferred Action to Unlawfully Present Aliens Legalize Their Status?

A grant of deferred action does not constitute "legalization," as that term is generally understood. In the immigration context, the term *legalization* is widely used to describe a process whereby persons who are unlawfully present are able to acquire legal status, typically as LPRs.[89] LPRs may generally acquire U.S. citizenship after a period of time if certain conditions are met.[90]

Aliens granted deferred action are generally seen as "lawfully present" for purposes of federal law.[91] This means that they do not acquire additional unlawful presence for application of the 3- and 10-year bars on the admissibility of aliens who have been unlawfully present in the United States for more than 180 days. Aliens granted deferred action may also be eligible for certain things—like the issuance of driver's licenses—that are made available, pursuant to federal, state, or local law, to persons who are "lawfully present" (or "legally residing") in the United States.[92] (See "Will aliens granted deferred action be eligible for public benefits?").

However, lawful presence is not the same as lawful status, and aliens granted deferred action lack lawful status.[93] As such, a grant of deferred action, in itself, will not result in an alien obtaining LPR status, a "green card," or citizenship, or the ability to sponsor family members for immigration benefits. Aliens granted deferred action could potentially have their status legalized by Congress in the future, though, as happened with earlier "groups" of aliens granted temporary relief from removal.[94]

Will Aliens Granted Deferred Action Be Eligible for Public Benefits?

As a general matter, aliens granted deferred action are not eligible for federal, state, or local public benefits because of the provisions of the Personal Responsibility and Work Opportunity Reconciliation Act (PRWORA) of 1996, as amended.[95] PRWORA established a definition of *qualified alien* that does not include aliens granted deferred action,[96] and generally barred aliens who are not qualified aliens from receiving federal, state, and local public benefits.[97]

Nonetheless, aliens granted deferred action could potentially be eligible for certain benefits—or things sometimes perceived as benefits—because aliens granted deferred action are seen as "lawfully present" (or "legally residing") in the United States. This is, in part, because one Congress cannot bind future Congresses.[98] Thus, despite PRWORA's restrictions upon the receipt of public benefits by aliens who are not included within its definition of "qualified aliens," subsequent Congresses have enacted legislation that provides for aliens' receipt of public benefits that is inconsistent with—and does not use the language of—PRWORA. For example, Section 214 of the Children's Health Insurance Program Reauthorization Act of 2009 (CHIPRA) gives states the option to provide Medicaid and Children's Health Insurance Program (CHIP) coverage to otherwise eligible children and pregnant women "who are lawfully residing in the United States,"[99] a phrase which has been taken to include aliens granted deferred action.[100] The Patient Protection and Affordable Care Act (ACA) of 2010 similarly permits persons who are "lawfully present" to participate in certain health care programs established under the act.[101] However, while *lawfully present* for purposes of ACA has generally been construed in the same way as *lawfully residing* for purposes of CHIPRA,[102] those granted deferred action through DACA have been deemed ineligible for certain benefits under ACA.[103] (As of the date of this report, the Administration does not appear to have formally addressed how aliens granted deferred action through the November initiatives will be treated for purposes of ACA.)

Another reason why aliens granted deferred action may be eligible for state and local benefits, in particular, is that PRWORA expressly contemplates states enacting legislation, subsequent to PRWORA's enactment, that "affirmatively provides" for "unlawfully present aliens" to receive state and local public benefits.[104] Numerous states have exercised this authority to enact legislation that makes at least some state or local public benefits available to either unlawfully present aliens or aliens who are not qualified aliens for purposes of PRWORA.[105]

In addition, it is important to note that PRWORA's definition of *public benefit* is limited to

> (A) any grant, contract, loan, professional license, or commercial license provided by [a government] agency ... or by appropriated funds ...; and
>
> (B) any retirement, welfare, health, disability, public or assisted housing, postsecondary education, food assistance, unemployment benefit, or any other similar benefit for which payments or assistance are provided to an individual, household, or family eligibility unit by [a government] agency ... or by appropriated funds.[106]

Given this definition, PRWORA has not been seen as barring the provision of certain benefits or services that some might characterize as public benefits—such as driver's licenses[107] or admission to public institutions of higher education[108]—but that are generally not seen as included within the definition of "public benefits" given by PRWORA.

Who Has Standing to Challenge the Administration's Initiatives?

The feasibility of legal challenges to the Obama Administration's actions will depend, in part, upon which specific actions are challenged and the legal bases for the challenge. However, regardless of the specifics of individual cases, standing requirements seem likely to pose a significant barrier for any legal challenge.

Standing requirements are concerned with who is a proper party to seek judicial relief from a federal court. They derive from Article III of the Constitution, which confines the jurisdiction of federal courts to actual "Cases" and "Controversies."[109] The case-or-controversy requirement has long been construed to restrict Article III courts to the adjudication of real, live disputes involving parties who have "a personal stake in the outcome of the controversy."[110] Parties seeking judicial relief from an Article III court must generally show three things in order to demonstrate standing: (1) they have suffered an "injury in fact" that is (a) concrete and particularized and (b) actual or imminent; (2) the injury is fairly traceable to the challenged action of the defendant; and (3) the injury is likely to be redressed by a favorable decision.[111]

"Taxpayer Standing"

Those whose sole injury is the government's alleged failure to follow the law are generally found to lack standing because this injury is not personal and particularized.[112] This is so regardless of whether the plaintiff alleges that his/her "tax dollars" can be seen as helping to fund the government's allegedly improper action or inaction.

Government Personnel

Government officers and employees, who have taken an oath to uphold the law, are generally found to lack standing so long as their only asserted injury is being forced to violate their oaths by implementing an allegedly unlawful policy or practice.[113] Instead, they must allege some separate and concrete adverse consequence that would flow from violating their oath, and courts have reached differing conclusions as to whether the possibility of being disciplined for obeying—or refusing to obey—allegedly unlawful orders suffices for purposes of standing, or whether such injury is "entirely speculative" and, therefore, lacking imminence.[114] In the case of the ICE officers who challenged DACA, the reviewing district court found that the plaintiffs had standing because of the possibility of such discipline. However, because such discipline constitutes an adverse employment action, the same court subsequently found that the plaintiffs' case is within the jurisdiction of the Merit Systems Protection Board (MSPB), not the court's.[115] (This decision has been appealed to the U.S. Court of Appeals for the Fifth Circuit, and it remains to be seen whether the district court's view as to jurisdiction is upheld.)

Members of Congress

Individual Members of Congress are generally seen to lack standing to challenge executive actions. In *Raines v. Byrd*, the Supreme Court held that, in order to obtain standing, an individual Member must assert either a personal injury, like the loss of his/her congressional seat, or an "institutional injury" that cannot be addressed by an extant legislative remedy.[116]

State Governments

In several prior cases, states sought to challenge the federal government's alleged failure to enforce immigration law on the grounds that this "failure" imposes costs upon the states, which must provide public benefits and services to aliens who, under this argument, would not have been present within the state had the federal government enforced the INA.[117] Some of these challenges have been rejected on standing grounds.[118] In other cases, the court either "presumed" or did not address the standing requirements,[119] but found that states' challenges presented a nonjusticiable political question.[120] (The political question doctrine embodies the notion that courts should refrain from deciding questions that the Constitution has entrusted to other branches of government.[121])

Economic Competitors

An argument has recently been advanced that U.S. workers whose wages or working conditions are adversely affected by increased competition from aliens permitted to work in the United States could show "competitor standing" and, thus, challenge the Obama Administration's actions.[122] This argument is, in part, based on a June 2014 decision wherein the U.S. Court of Appeals for the District of Columbia Circuit found that U.S. persons working as herders had standing to challenge the DOL's decision to issue certain guidance as to the wages and hours of foreign herders without notice-and-comment rulemaking because DOL's action caused "increased competition for jobs in their industry."[123] However, this case could potentially be distinguished from a challenge to the Obama Administration's deferred actions, in particular, because the INA expressly requires the executive branch to take certain steps to protect U.S. workers from foreign competition when issuing certain types of nonimmigrant visas, like those at issue in the June decision.[124] There do not appear to be any such requirements as to the executive's determination to issue employment authorization documents to aliens who do not hold employment-based visas.[125]

Is There Historical Precedent for the Administration's Actions?

Competing arguments have been made as to whether there is historical precedent for the Obama Administration's actions, particularly in granting deferred action to certain aliens brought to the United States as children and to the parents of U.S. citizen or LPR children.[126] Such arguments are shaped, in part, by which historical actions are viewed as analogous to the current ones.

The executive has historically exercised its prosecutorial or enforcement discretion, delegated discretion, and/or discretion in interpreting and applying statutes to provide certain relief from removal to individual aliens who share certain characteristics and could, thus, be said to form a group or category.[127] At different times, such relief has been made available under the rubric of parole (or refugee parole), extended voluntary departure (EVD), indefinite voluntary departure (IVD), deferred enforced departure (DED), temporary protected status (TPS), and deferred action. However, the shared name given to such actions can mask important differences in the legal basis for particular grants of discretion, among other things. For example, not all grants of parole to aliens in the 1960s should be seen as exercises of prosecutorial or enforcement discretion since Congress enacted legislation in 1960 that temporarily provided the executive with express statutory authority to parole "refugees" into the United States.[128] Likewise, in some cases, Congress has expressly adopted legislation encouraging the executive to exercise particular forms of prosecutorial or enforcement discretion in certain cases, which could potentially be said to indicate congressional "approval" of the executive's exercise of this authority.[129]

The temporary relief from removal granted to unlawfully present aliens that some have asserted most closely resembles the Obama Administration's deferred action initiatives[130]—particularly in terms of the percentage of the unauthorized alien population affected—are the so-called "Family Fairness" initiatives of 1987 and 1990. In those cases, the Reagan and George H.W. Bush Administrations, respectively, granted indefinite voluntary departure (IVD) and employment authorization to certain immediate relatives of aliens who had legalized their status pursuant to IRCA.[131] (These relatives were themselves ineligible for legalization under IRCA for various reasons.) The Obama Administration's 2014 deferred action initiatives can be likened to the Family Fairness initiatives in that they involve the granting of temporary relief from removal and work authorization to certain unlawfully present aliens based, in part, on humanitarian factors. However, certain differences could also be noted between the current and earlier initiatives, including that (1) the Reagan and Bush Administrations did not establish a centralized process whereby aliens could apply for relief from removal, instead permitting regional officials to grant relief; (2) some aliens who were denied relief through the Family Fairness initiatives were reportedly placed in removal proceedings,[132] something that has not been reported with DACA;[133] and (3) the Family Fairness initiatives were preceded (and followed) by the enactment of legislation legalizing certain unlawfully present aliens, whereas Congress has enacted no such legislation here.[134] How much weight is given to these similarities or dissimilarities may ultimately depend upon one's views as to the permissibility and/or desirability of the current initiatives.

End Notes

[1] For a transcript of the President's address, see http://www.whitehouse.gov/issues/immigration/immigration-action# (last accessed: Nov. 22, 2014).

[2] See generally Dep't of Homeland Security (DHS), Fixing Our Broken Immigration System Through Executive Action - Key Facts, Nov. 21, 2014, available at http://www.dhs.gov/immigration-action?utm_source=hp_feature& utm_medium=web&utm_campaign=dhs_hp; Dep't of Labor (DOL), Immigration Fact Sheets, available at http://www.dol.gov/dol/fact-sheet/immigration/ (last accessed: Nov. 21, 2014).

[3] See DHS Secretary Janet Napolitano, Exercising Prosecutorial Discretion with Respect to Individuals Who Came to the United States as Children, June 15, 2012 (copy on file with the author).

[4] See, e.g., Crane v. Napolitano, Amended Complaint, No. 3:12-cv-03247-O, filed Oct. 10, 2012 (N.D. Tex.) (lawsuit challenging DACA and arguing that the initiative is, among other things, contrary to specific provisions of the INA and the Executive's constitutional responsibility to "take care" that the laws are faithfully executed); Robert J. Delahunty & John C. Yoo, Dream On: The Obama Administration's Nonenforcement of Immigration Laws, the DREAM Act, and the Take Care Clause, 91 TEX. L. REV. 781 (2013) (arguing that the DACA initiative is inconsistent with the Executive's constitutional duties, and that the President may not purposefully refrain from enforcing federal statutes against broad categories of persons "in ordinary, noncritical circumstances").

[5] See, e.g., Shoba Sivaprasad Wadhia, In Defense of DACA, Deferred Action, and the DREAM Act, 91 TEX. L. REV. 59 (2013) (asserting that DACA is a constitutionally justified attempt by the Executive "to enforce congressionally mandated priorities" by focusing limited resources on the removal of aliens designated as a "high-priority" for removal); David A. Martin, A Defense of Immigration-Enforcement Discretion: The Legal and Policy Flaws of Kris Kobach's Latest Crusade, 122 YALE L.J. ONLINE 167 (2012) (arguing that DACA is consistent with the INA and with previous exercises of enforcement discretion by immigration officials).

[6] DHS Secretary Jeh Charles Johnson, Memorandum, Southern Border and Approaches Campaign, Nov. 20, 2014, at 1 (copy on file with the author).

[7] Id. at 2.

[8] See, e.g., Unauthorized Immigrants: How Pew Research Counts Them and What We Know about Them, Pew Research Center, Apr. 17, 2013, available at http://www.pewresearch.org/2013/04/17/unauthorized-immigrants-howpew-research-counts-them-and-what-we-know-about-them/.

[9] DHS Secretary Jeh Charles Johnson, Memorandum, Exercising Prosecutorial Discretion with Respect to Individuals Who Came to the United States as Children and with Respect to Certain Individuals Whose Parents [sic] Are U.S. Citizens or Permanent Residents, Nov. 20, 2014 (copy on file with the author).

[10] See DHS Secretary Janet Napolitano, Exercising Prosecutorial Discretion with Respect to Individuals Who Came to the United States as Children, June 15, 2012, at 2 (copy on file with the author).

[11] Id.

[12] Exercising Prosecutorial Discretion, supra note 9. See also DHS, USCIS, Executive Actions on Immigration, last updated: Nov. 20, 2014, available at http://www.uscis.gov/immigrationaction.

[13] Id. The Administration has, however, noted that a grant of deferred action through DACA could be revoked. See U.S. Citizenship & Immigr. Servs. (USCIS), Consideration of Deferred Action for Childhood Arrivals Process: Frequently Asked Questions, last updated Oct. 23, 2014, available at http://www.uscis.gov/humanitarian/consideration-deferredaction-childhood-arrivals-process/frequently-asked-questions.

[14] Exercising Prosecutorial Discretion, supra note 9.

[15] Id.

[16] See DHS, ICE, How to Seek Prosecutorial Discretion from ICE, available at http://www.ice.gov/immigrationaction (last accessed: Nov. 21, 2014).

[17] 8 C.F.R. §274a.12(c)(14). Under these regulations, the "basic criteria" for establishing economic necessity are the federal poverty guidelines. See 8 C.F.R. §274a.12(e).

[18] DHS Secretary Jeh Charles Johnson, Memorandum, Policies for the Apprehension, Detention and Removal of Undocumented Immigrants, Nov. 20, 2014 (copies on file with the author). Two earlier memoranda by then-Director of ICE John Morton articulating civil immigration enforcement priorities were expressly rescinded and superseded. Id.

[19] DHS Secretary Jeh Charles Johnson, Memorandum, Secure Communities, Nov. 20, 2014 (copies on file with the author).

[20] Cf. DHS, ICE, Secure Communities: The Basics, available at http://www. ice. gov/ secure_ communities (last accessed: Nov. 23, 2014).

[21] The primary means that DHS had relied upon to request such holds by states and localities—so-called "immigration detainers" (Form I-247)—have recently been the subject of extensive litigation. In March 2014, the U.S. Court of Appeals for the Third Circuit ruled that federal law does not require states and localities to hold aliens who are subject to immigration detainers, and that any attempt to require states and localities to do so would run afoul of the "anti-commandeering" principles of the Tenth Amendment. See Galarza v. Szalczyk, 745 F.3d 634 (3d Cir. 2014). More recently, in April 2014, a federal district court found that states and localities must have probable cause to hold an alien pursuant to a detainer; the mere filing of a detainer does not provide the requisite legal authority for such holds. See Miranda-Olivares v. Clackamas County, No. 3:12-cv-02317-ST, 2014 U.S. Dist. LEXIS 50340 (D. Or., Apr. 11, 2014). For more information, see generally CRS Report R42690, Immigration Detainers: Legal Issues, by Kate M. Manuel.

[22] DHS Secretary Jeh Charles Johnson, Memorandum, Directive to Provide Consistency Regarding Advance Parole, Nov. 20, 2014, available at http://www.dhs. Gov /sites/default/files/publications/14_1120_memo_arrabally.pdf.

[23] DHS Secretary Jeh Charles Johnson, Memorandum, Families of U.S. Armed Forces Members and Enlistees, Nov. 20, 2014 (copy on file with the author).

[24] A grant of parole in place could potentially entitle such aliens to other types of relief from removal. See, e.g., INA §245(a), 8 U.S.C. §1255(a) (permitting adjustment to LPR status for certain aliens who have been admitted or paroled).

[25] DHS Secretary Jeh Charles Johnson, Memorandum, Policies Supporting U.S. High-Skilled Businesses and Workers, Nov. 20, 2014, at 1 (copy on file with the author). The memorandum also directs USCIS to continue with the promulgation of a proposed rule extending work authorization to the spouses of H-1B visa holders who have been approved for an employment-based immigrant visa, as well as the development of proposed guidance

to "strengthen and improve" processing of various employment-based non-immigrant visas. Id.

[26] Id. at 2. Ways to ensure that all available immigrant visas are used each year are also to be explored by the newly established interagency task force on modernizing and streamlining the immigrant visa system, discussed below. See President Barack Obama, Memorandum, Modernizing and Streamlining the U.S. Immigrant Visa System for the 21st Century, Nov. 21, 2014 (copy on file with the author).

[27] See, e.g., USCIS, Responding to Your Comments on Visa Numbers, Preference Categories, and Spillover, Mar. 30, 2010, available at http://blog.uscis.gov/2010/03/visa-numbers.html.

[28] See, e.g., Patrick Thibodeau, Obama's Options for Tech Immigration Take Shape, COMPUTERWORLD, Aug. 20, 2014, available at http://www.computerworld.com/ article/ 2598332/technology-law-regulation/obama-s-options-for-techimmigration-take-shape.html. The INA provides that any unused employment-based immigrant visas from one year are available for use as family-based immigrant visas the following year, and vice versa. INA §201(c) & (d), 8 U.S.C. §1151(c) & (d). Thus, some have questioned the significance of "recapture" proposals. See, e.g., Numbers USA, Visa "Recapture," available at https://www.numbersusa.com/content/files/pdf/Fact%20Sheet%20Visa%20Recapture.pdf (last accessed: Nov. 22, 2014).

[29] Policies Supporting U.S. High-Skilled Businesses and Workers, supra note 25, at 2.

[30] Id. at 3.

[31] See, e.g., Immigration and Naturalization Service (INS), Nonimmigrant Classes: F-1 Academic Students, 52 Fed. Reg. 13223 (Apr. 22, 1987).

[32] See DHS, ICE, Extending Period of Optional Practical Training by 17 Months for F-1 Nonimmigrant Students With STEM Degrees and Expanding Cap-Gap Relief for All F-1 Students With Pending H-1B Petitions, 73 Fed. Reg. 18944 (Apr. 8, 2008).

[33] See cases discussed infra note 125 and accompanying text.

[34] Policies Supporting U.S. High-Skilled Businesses and Workers, supra note 25, at 2.

[35] While the Executive has generally based determinations as to whether to parole aliens into the United States on "urgent humanitarian reasons," also noted in INA §212(d)(5)(A), there have instances when the Executive considered labor-related factors when granting parole. See "A Brief History of the Executive Branch's Parole of Aliens into the United States," in CRS Report R43782, Executive Discretion as to Immigration: Legal Overview, by Kate M. Manuel and Michael John Garcia.

[36] The issuance of U visas is generally conditioned, in part, on a designated law enforcement agency "certifying" or corroborating that aliens who are victims of specified criminal offenses have assisted law enforcement or other government officials in the investigation or prosecution of those crimes. Such certification is not required with T visas, but can be helpful in obtaining a T visa.

[37] See generally Policies Supporting U.S. High-Skilled Businesses and Workers, supra note 25; Modernizing and Streamlining the U.S. Immigrant Visa System for the 21st Century, supra note 26; DOL Secretary Thomas E. Perez, Fact Sheet, Department of Labor to Pursue Modernized Recruitment and Application Requirements for the PERM Program (copy on file with the author); DOL Secretary Thomas E. Perez, Fact Sheet, The Department of Labor's Wage and House Division Will Expand Its Support of Victims of Human Trafficking and Other Crimes Seeking Immigration Relief from DHS (copy on file with the author).

[38] DHS Secretary Jeh Charles Johnson, Memorandum, Expansion of the Provisional Waiver Program, Nov. 20, 2014 (copy on file with the author).

[39] See generally CRS Legal Sidebar WSLG385, Provisional Waivers of the Three- and Ten-Year Bars to Admissibility to Be Granted to Certain Unlawfully Present Aliens, by Kate M. Manuel.

[40] INA §212(a)(9)(B)(i)(I)-(II), 8 U.S.C. §1182(a)(9)(B)(i)(I)-(II). The 3-year bar applies to aliens who have been unlawfully present for more than 180 days but less than 1 year. The 10-year bar applies to aliens who have been unlawfully present for 1 year or longer. Longer or permanent bars could apply to certain aliens, depending upon their circumstances. See, e.g., INA §212(a)(9)(A), 8 U.S.C. §1182(a)(9)(A) (certain aliens barred from entry for 20 years).

[41] INA §212(a)(9)(B)(v), 8 U.S.C. §1182(a)(9)(B)(v).

[42] See DHS, USCIS, Provisional Unlawful Presence Waivers of Inadmissibility for Certain Immediate Relatives, 78 Fed. Reg. 536, 542 (Jan. 3, 2013) (noting that DHS initially limited eligibility for provisional waivers to immediate relatives of U.S. citizens "not only because the immigrant visas for this category are always available, but also because it is consistent with Congress' policy choice to prioritize family reunification of immediate relatives of U.S. citizens").

[43] DHS Secretary Jeh Charles Johnson, Memorandum, Personnel Reforms for Immigration and Customs Enforcement Officers, Nov. 20, 2014 (copy on file with the author).

[44] DHS Secretary Jeh Charles Johnson, Memorandum, Policies to Promote and Increase Access to U.S. Citizenship, Nov. 20, 2014 (copy on file with the author) (directing USCIS to begin accepting credit cards for paying naturalization fees; consider the feasibility of partial waivers of naturalization fees in its next biennial fee study (currently only total waivers are granted); and launch a "comprehensive media campaign" to promote naturalization).

[45] President Barack Obama, Memorandum, Creating Welcoming Communities and Fully Integrating Immigrants and Refugees, Nov. 21, 2014 (copy on file with the author).

[46] DOL Secretary Thomas E. Perez, Fact Sheet, Establishment of Interagency Working Group for the Consistent Enforcement of Federal Labor, Employment and Immigration Laws (copy on file with the author).

[47] See supra notes 26 and 45 and accompanying text.

[48] See INS, Office of the Commissioner, Memorandum, Family Fairness: Guidelines for Voluntary Departure under 8 C.F.R. 242.5 for the Ineligible Spouses and Children of Legalized Aliens, Feb. 2, 1990 (copy on file with the author).

[49] See President William J. Clinton, Memorandum for the Attorney General, Measures Regarding Certain Liberians in the United States, Sept. 28, 2000 (copy on file with the author).

[50] See, e.g., Hotel & Rest. Employees Union Local 25 v. Smith, 846 F.2d 1499, 1510-11 (D.C. Cir. 1988); BarahonaGomez v. Reno, 236 F.3d 1115, 1119 n.3 (9th Cir. 2001); Johnson v. INS, 962 F.2d 574, 579 (7th Cir. 1992); Carmona Martinez v. Ashcroft, 118 Fed. App'x 238, 239 (9th Cir. 2004); Matter of Yauri, 25 I. & N. Dec. 103 (BIA 2009); Matter of Singh, 21 I. & N. Dec. 427 (BIA 1996); Matter of Luviano-Rodriguez, 21 I. & N. Dec. 235 (BIA 1996); Matter of Quintero, 18 I. & N. Dec. 348 (BIA 1982); ICE Director John Morton, Exercising Prosecutorial Discretion Consistent with the Civil Immigration Enforcement Priorities of the Agency for the Apprehension, Detention, and Removal of Aliens, June 17, 2011, at 2-3; ICE Director John Morton, Civil Immigration Enforcement: Priorities for the Apprehension, Detention, and Removal of Aliens, Mar. 2, 2011, at 3; ICE Director John Morton, Prosecutorial Discretion: Certain Victims, Witnesses, and Plaintiffs, June 17, 2011, at 2; ICE Principal Legal Advisor William J. Howard, Prosecutorial Discretion, Oct. 24, 2005, at 2; INS Commissioner Doris Meissner, Exercising Prosecutorial Discretion, Nov. 7, 2000, at 2. (Copies of all of these memoranda are on file with the author).

[51] For further discussion as to the basis for the Executive's prosecutorial discretion, see the section titled "Prosecutorial Discretion Generally," in CRS Report R42924, Prosecutorial Discretion in Immigration Enforcement: Legal Issues, by Kate M. Manuel and Todd Garvey.

[52] The INA uses the phrase "deferred action" three times, but only in very specific contexts, none of which are relevant to DACA or the November 20, 2014, initiatives. See 8 U.S.C. §1151 note (addressing the extension of posthumous benefits to certain surviving spouses, children, and parents); INA §204(a)(1)(D)(i)(IV), 8 U.S.C. §1154(a)(1)(D)(i)(IV) ("Any [victim of domestic violence] described in subclause (III) and any derivative child of a petition described in clause (ii) is eligible for deferred action and work authorization."); INA §237(d)(2), 8 U.S.C. §1227(d)(2) (denial of a request for an administrative stay of removal does not preclude the alien from applying for deferred action).

[53] See generally U.S. Department of Justice, United States Attorneys' Manual, §9-27.110(B) (2002).

[54] INA §274A(h)(3), 8 U.S.C. §1324a(h)(3).

[55] 8 C.F.R. §274a.12(c)(14). Under these regulations, the "basic criteria" for establishing "economic necessity" are the federal poverty guidelines. See 8 C.F.R. §274a.12(e). When first promulgated in 1987, these regulations were challenged through the administrative process on the grounds that they exceeded the INS's authority. See INS, Employment Authorization; Classes of Aliens Eligible, 52 Fed. Reg. 46092 (Dec. 4, 1987). Specifically, the challengers asserted that the statutory language referring to aliens "authorized to be ... employed by this chapter or by the Attorney General" did not give the Attorney General authority to grant work authorization "except to those aliens who have already been granted specific authorization by the Act." Id. Had this argument prevailed, the authority of the INS and, later, DHS to grant work authorization to beneficiaries of deferred action would have been in doubt, because the INA does not expressly authorize the grant of EADs to such persons. However, the INS rejected this argument on the grounds that the only logical way to interpret this phrase is that Congress, being fully aware of the Attorney General's authority to promulgate regulations, and approving of the manner in which he has exercised that authority in this matter, defined "unauthorized alien" in such fashion as to exclude aliens who have been authorized employment by the Attorney General through the regulatory process, in addition to those who are authorized employment by statute.

[56] It should be noted, however, that the determination as to whether to grant parole to individual aliens has sometimes been characterized as an act of prosecutorial discretion. See, e.g., Assa'ad v. U.S. Attorney General, 332 F.3d 1321, 1339 (11th Cir. 2003); Matter of Artigas, 23 I. & N. Dec. 99 (BIA 2001) (Filppu, J., dissenting).

[57] For further discussion of constraints based on historical precedent and other factors, see CRS Report R43782, Executive Discretion as to Immigration: Legal Overview, by Kate M. Manuel and Michael John Garcia.

[58] 467 U.S. 837, 842-43 (1984).

[59] Id. at 843.

[60] See, e.g., Morton v. Ruiz, 415 U.S. 199, 231 (1974) ("The power of an administrative agency to administer a congressionally created and funded program necessarily requires the formulation of policy and the making of rules to fill any gap left, implicitly or explicitly, by Congress."). The degree of deference afforded to particular executive branch interpretations can vary depending upon the facts and circumstances of the case, including whether the interpretation is a "formal" one adopted through notice-and-comment rulemaking or case-by-case adjudication. See, e.g., Christensen v. Harris County, 529 U.S. 576, 587 (2000)

("Interpretations such as those in opinion letters - like interpretations contained in policy statements, agency manuals, and enforcement guidelines, all of which lack the force of law - do not warrant Chevron-style deference."). Instead, such "informal" interpretations may be afforded a lesser degree of deference that depends upon various factors including "the degree of the agency's care, its consistency, formality, and relative expertness, and ... the persuasiveness of the agency's position," as well as the "writer's thoroughness, logic, and expertise, its fit with prior interpretations, and any other source of weight." United States v. Mead Corp., 533 U.S. 218, 228, 235 (2001); see also Skidmore v. Swift, 323 U.S. 134 (1944).

[61] See infra note 88 and accompanying text.

[62] CRS Legislative Attorney Michael John Garcia authored this section of the report, and questions about it should be directed to him. For a more extensive analysis of the parameters of executive discretion in the enforcement federal law, see CRS Report R43708, The Take Care Clause and Executive Discretion in the Enforcement of Law, by Todd Garvey.

[63] U.S. Const., Art. II, §3.

[64] DOJ, Office of Legal Counsel, The Department of Homeland Security's Authority to Prioritize Removal of Certain Aliens Unlawfully Present in the United States and to Defer Removal of Others, Nov. 20, 2014 (copy on file with the author) (characterizing components of the Administration's immigration initiative primarily as an exercise of the Executive's independent discretionary authority). It should be noted, however, that certain actions taken with respect to persons granted deferred action are based on express statutory authority, as previously discussed. See "What is the legal authority for the Administration's actions?".

[65] See generally DOJ, United States Attorneys' Manual, §9-27.110(B) (2002).

[66] See, e.g., Bordenkircher v. Hayes, 434 U.S. 357, 364 (1978) ("In our system, so long as the prosecutor has probable cause to believe that the accused committed an offense defined by statute, the decision whether or not to prosecute, and what charge to file or bring before a grand jury, generally rests entirely in his discretion."); U.S. Attorneys' Manuel, supra note 65 (discussing prosecutorial discretion in the criminal context and citing numerous court rulings recognizing the Executive as possessing broad discretionary authority in deciding whether to pursue criminal charges).

[67] See Arizona v. United States, 132 S. Ct. 2492, 2498 (2012) ("A principal feature of the removal system is the broad discretion entrusted to immigration officials."); Reno v. American-Arab Anti-Discrimination Committee, 525 U.S. 471, 490 (1999) (finding that the various prudential concerns that prompt deference to the executive branch's determinations as to whether to prosecute criminal offenses are "greatly magnified in the deportation context"). See also United States ex rel. Knauff v. Shaughnessy, 338 U.S. 537, 543 (1950) (noting that immigration is a "field where flexibility and the adaptation of the congressional policy to infinitely variable conditions constitute the essence of the program").

[68] See Heckler v. Chaney, 470 U.S. 821, 831 (1985) (finding that agency's non-enforcement decision was committed to agency discretion and not reviewable under the Administrative Procedure Act, and observing that "This Court has recognized on several occasions over many years that an agency's decision not to prosecute or enforce, whether through civil or criminal process, is a decision generally committed to an agency's absolute discretion....This recognition of the existence of discretion is attributable in no small part to the general unsuitability for judicial review of agency decisions to refuse enforcement."). A court's determination that agency action is not subject to judicial review does not necessarily constitute an endorsement of the lawfulness of executive action, but may simply

be due to the court finding that it lacks a manageable standard or is otherwise ill-equipped to assess the propriety of the action. See CRS Report RL30352, War Powers Litigation Initiated by Members of Congress Since the Enactment of the War Powers Resolution, by Michael John Garcia (discussing instances where courts have dismissed on procedural grounds legal challenges to military action conducted without statutory authorization).

[69] See, e.g., Heckler, 470 U.S. at 831-833 (identifying factors informing the scope of enforcement discretion available to the Executive); Smith v. Meese, 821 F.2d 1484, 1492 n.4 (11th Cir. 1987) ("[T]he exercise of prosecutorial discretion, like the exercise of Executive discretion generally, is subject to statutory and constitutional limits enforceable through judicial review ...") (quoting Nader v. Saxbe, 497 F.2d 676, 679 n.19 (D.C. Cir.1974)); OLC Opinion on Executive Immigration Action, supra note 64, at 4 ("Immigration officials' discretion in enforcing the laws is not, however, unlimited. Limits on enforcement discretion are both implicit in, and fundamental to, the Constitution's allocation of governmental powers between the two political branches.").

[70] See Crowley Caribbean Transport, Inc. v. Pena, 37 F.3d 671, 677 (D.C. Cir. 1994) (distinguishing the nonreviewability of a "single-shot non-enforcement decision" from a "general enforcement policy," which may be reviewable in some contexts).

[71] Motor Vehicle Mfrs. Ass'n v. State Farm Mut. Auto. Ins. Co., 463 U.S. 29, 43 (1983).

[72] See Heckler, 470 U.S. at 833 n.4 (distinguishing agency non-enforcement decisions which are presumed to be shielded from judicial review from those where "the agency has 'consciously and expressly adopted a general policy' that is so extreme as to amount to an abdication of its statutory responsibilities," and suggesting that judicial review of the latter type of actions could be available under the Administrative Procedure Act because such a decision had not been committed to agency discretion) (quoting Adams v. Richardson, 480 F.2d 1159, 1162 (D.C. Cir. 1973) (en banc)).

[73] See OLC Opinion on Executive Immigration Action, supra note 64, at 30 (Administration officials estimating that nearly 4 million unlawfully present alien parents of U.S. citizens or LPRs could receive deferred action under the new initiative); Alicia Patterson, Graphic: What Is President Obama's Immigration Plan?, N.Y. TIMES, available at http://www.nytimes.com/interactive/2014/11/20/us/2014-11-20-immigration.html?_r=0 (last accessed Nov. 23, 2014) (citing 2012 data from the Migration Policy Institute, and estimating that 4.5 million unlawfully present aliens could be eligible for deferred action under the Administration's new initiative, in addition to 1.2 million persons already eligible to obtain deferred action under DACA).

[74] See, e.g., Crane v. Napolitano, Amended Complaint, No. 3:12-cv-03247-O, filed Oct. 10, 2012 (N.D. Tex.) (lawsuit challenging DACA and arguing that the initiative is contrary to certain provisions of the INA and the Executive's constitutional responsibility to that the laws are faithfully executed); Dream On, supra note 4 (arguing that the DACA initiative is inconsistent with the Executive's constitutional duties, and that the President may not purposefully refrain from enforcing federal statutes against broad categories of persons "in ordinary, noncritical circumstances").

[75] INA §§212(a)(6)(A), 8 U.S.C. §1182(a)(6)(A) (aliens present without admission or parole are generally removable; INA §237(a)(1), 8 U.S.C. §§ 1182(a)(6)(A), 1227(a)(1) (aliens who obtained admission through fraud or misrepresentation, or who overstay or otherwise violate the terms of a nonimmigrant visa, are removable).

[76] For example, under INA §240A, certain removable aliens may obtain cancellation of removal and adjust immigration status if their removal would cause "exceptional and extremely unusual hardship" to certain family members who are U.S. citizens or LPRs. No more than

4,000 aliens may be granted such relief in any fiscal year. 8 U.S.C. §1229b. Some inadmissibility grounds may be waived on account of "hardship" caused to immediate family members who are U.S. citizens or LPRs. See generally CRS Report R43782, Executive Discretion as to Immigration: Legal Overview, by Kate M. Manuel and Michael John Garcia, at "Waivers of Grounds of Inadmissibility."

[77] See supra note 52.

[78] See OLC Opinion on Executive Immigration Action, supra note 64, at 1, 9 (noting that DHS claims to have the resources to remove fewer than 400,000 unlawfully present aliens—out of a population of approximately 11 million— from the United States each year).

[79] Id. at 10-11 (characterizing DHS's announced enforcement priorities as consistent with various provisions of the INA, as well as with recent funding measures, including a provision of the Department of Homeland Security Appropriations Act, 2014, which directs DHS to "prioritize the identification and removal of aliens convicted of a crime by the severity of that crime.").

[80] See supra "What is the legal authority for the Administration's actions?" (discussing, among other things, DHS's statutory authority to grant work authorization to aliens present in the United States without legal immigration status).

[81] The memorandum outlining the expanded deferred action initiative expressly states that, although "immigration officers will be provided with specific eligibility criteria for deferred action, ... the ultimate judgment as to whether an immigrant is granted deferred action will be determined on a case-by-case basis." Exercising Prosecutorial Discretion, supra note 9, at 5. Similarly, the memorandum outlining DHS's enforcement priorities does not prohibit enforcement action against aliens not categorized as priorities for removal. Policies for the Apprehension, Detention and Removal of Undocumented Immigrants, supra note 18, at 4 ("Nothing in this memorandum should be construed to prohibit or discourage the apprehension, detention, or removal of aliens unlawfully in the United States who are not identified as priorities herein.").

[82] See OLC Opinion on Executive Immigration Action, supra note 64, at 12-20 (discussing historical use of deferred action and claiming that "Congress has long been aware of the practice of granting deferred action, including in its categorical variety, and of its salient features; and it has never acted to disapprove or limit the practice"). See also Dames & Moore v. Regan, 453 U.S. 654, 686 (1981) ("Past practice does not, by itself, create power, but 'long-continued practice, known to and acquiesced in by Congress, would raise a presumption that the [action] had been [taken] in pursuance of its consent.... '") (quoting United States v. Midwest Oil Co., 236 U.S. 459, 474 (1915)).

[83] See supra notes 58-60 and accompanying text.

[84] Crane v. Napolitano, No. 3:12-cv-03247-O, 2013 U.S. Dist. LEXIS 57788, *27-*39 (N.D. Tex., Apr. 23, 2013). Others, however, have argued that this interpretation misreads Section 235 and misunderstands the legislative history of these provisions of the INA. See A Defense of Immigration-Enforcement Discretion, supra note 5. DHS has also attempted to counter this view by noting the Executive has historically not construed Section 235 in this way. Both DOJ/DHS and those who claim it lacks discretion construe the first two provisions of Section 235—aliens present without admission being deemed applicants for admission, and applicants for admission being inspected—as applying to both (1) "arriving aliens" at a port-of-entry and (2) aliens who are present in the United States without inspection. However, DOJ/DHS have differed from proponents of the view that DHS lacks discretion in that DOJ/DHS have construed the third provision—regarding detention for removal proceedings—as applying only to arriving aliens, not aliens who are present

without inspection. See generally INS, Inspection and Expedited Removal of Aliens; Detention and Removal of Aliens; Conduct of Removal Proceedings; Asylum Procedures, 62 Fed. Reg. 10312, 10357 (Mar. 6, 1997) (codified at 8 C.F.R. §235.3(c)); INS, Inspection and Expedited Removal of Aliens; Detention and Removal of Aliens; Conduct of Removal Proceedings; Asylum Procedures, 62 Fed. Reg. 444, 444-46 (Jan. 3, 1997). This difference appears to have arisen, in part, because the agencies have emphasized the phrase "aliens seeking admission" in the third provision, and reasoned that only arriving aliens at ports-of-entry can be said to seek admission.

[85] See INA §235(a)(1), (a)(3), & (b)(2)(A), 8 U.S.C. §1225(a)(1), (a)(3), & (b)(2)(A). Shall has been construed to indicate mandatory agency action in some cases. See, e.g., Lopez v. Davis, 531 U.S. 230, 241 (2001) ("Congress' use of the permissive 'may' in §3621(e)(2)(B) contrasts with the legislators' use of a mandatory 'shall' in the very same section."). However, in other cases, agencies have been seen to have discretion in determining whether to enforce particular statutes that use the word shall. See, e.g., Heckler, 470 U.S. at 835 (describing a statute which stated that certain food, drugs, or cosmetics "shall be liable to be proceeded against" as "framed in the permissive").

[86] Crane v. Napolitano, No. 3:12-cv-03247-O, 2013 U.S. Dist. LEXIS 187005 (July 31, 2013).

[87] Moreover, even if the district court's interpretation were adopted, an argument could be made that the provisions of the INA discussed by the district court require only that arriving aliens be placed in removal proceedings, not that removal proceedings be pursued to a decision on the merits or until the alien is removed, if s/he is found removable.

[88] 8 U.S.C. §1182(a)(9)(B)(v) (emphases added).

[89] Cf. Merriam-Webster Online, Legalize, available at http://www.merriam-webster.com/dictionary/legalize (last accessed: Nov. 22, 2014).

[90] See INA §311, 8 U.S.C. §1422.

[91] See, e.g., Frequently Asked Questions, supra note 13 ("An individual who has received deferred action is authorized by DHS to be present in the United States, and is therefore considered by DHS to be lawfully present.").

[92] See generally CRS Report R43452, Unlawfully Present Aliens, Driver's Licenses, and Other State-Issued ID: Select Legal Issues, by Kate M. Manuel and Michael John Garcia; CRS Legal Sidebar WSLG1057, 9th Circuit Decision Enables DACA Beneficiaries—and Other Aliens Granted Deferred Action—to Get Arizona Driver's Licenses, by Kate M. Manuel.

[93] See Frequently Asked Questions, supra note 13 ("[D]eferred action does not confer lawful status ... ").

[94] See, e.g., Cuban Refugees Adjustment of Status Act, P.L.89-732, 80 Stat. 1161 (Nov. 2, 1966) (providing for certain Cuban parolees to become LPRs); Hungarian Refugees Relief Act, P.L. 85-559, 72 Stat. 419 (July 25, 1958) (similar).

[95] P.L. 104-193, tit. IV, §§401-435, 110 Stat. 2261-2276 (Aug. 22, 1996) (generally codified, as amended, in 8 U.S.C. §§1601-1646). For more on PRWORA, see generally CRS Report R43221, Noncitizen Eligibility for Public Benefits: Legal Issues , by Kate M. Manuel.

[96] See 8 U.S.C. §1641(b)(1)-(7) (defining qualified alien to encompass: LPRs; aliens granted asylum; refugees; aliens paroled into the United States for a period of at least one year; aliens whose deportation is being withheld; aliens granted conditional entry; and Cuban and Haitian entrants). Certain aliens who have been subject to domestic violence are also treated as qualified aliens for purposes of PRWORA. See 8 U.S.C. §1641(c).

[97] See 8 U.S.C. §1611(a) (federal public benefits); 8 U.S.C. §1621(a) (state and local public benefits).

[98] See United States v. Winstar Corp., 518 U.S. 839, 872 (1996) (quoting, in support of the proposition "that one legislature may not bind the legislative authority of its successors," 1 W. Blackstone, COMMENTARIES ON THE LAWS OF ENGLAND 90 (1765) ("Acts of parliament derogatory from the power of subsequent parliaments bind not.... Because the legislature, being in truth the sovereign power, is always of equal, always of absolute authority: it acknowledges no superior upon earth, which the prior legislature must have been, if it's [sic] ordinances could bind the present parliament.").

[99] P.L. 111-3, §214(a), 123 Stat. 56 (Feb. 4, 2009) (codified at 42 U.S.C. §1396b(v)(4)(A)-(B)).

[100] Centers for Medicare & Medicaid Services, Medicaid and CHIP Coverage of "Lawfully Residing" Children and Pregnant Women, July 1, 2010 (copy on file with the author).

[101] See, e.g., P.L. 111-148, §1101(d)(1), 124 Stat. 142 (Mar. 23, 2010) (temporary high risk health insurance pools for uninsured individuals with preexisting conditions); id., at §1312(f)(3), 124 Stat. 184 (health care exchanges).

[102] See, e.g., Department of the Treasury, Health Insurance Premium Tax Credit: Final Regulations, 77 Fed. Reg. 30377, 30387 (May 23, 2012) ("Lawfully present has the same meaning as in 45 CFR 155.20."). Section 155.20 of Title 45, in turn, defines lawfully present as qualified aliens; nonimmigrants who have not violated the terms of their status; certain aliens paroled into the United States; and aliens granted deferred action or deferred enforced departure, among others.

[103] See, e.g., Department of Health & Human Servs., Center for Medicaid & CHIP Servs., Individuals with Deferred Action for Childhood Arrivals, Aug. 28, 2012 (copy on file with the author).

[104] 8 U.S.C. §1621(d).

[105] See, e.g., Pimentel v. Dreyfus, 670 F.3d 1096, 1101 (9th Cir. 2012) (Washington statute extending food stamp benefits to aliens who lost their eligibility for federal food stamps due to PRWORA); Ehrlich v. Perez, 908 A.2d 1220 (Md. 2006) (Maryland statute providing comprehensive medical care to qualified aliens who had not been present in the United States in that status for the requisite period of time to receive federal means-tested public benefits).

[106] U.S.C. §1611(c)(1) (federal public benefits); 8 U.S.C. §1621(c)(1) (state and local public benefits).

[107] See sources cited supra note 92.

[108] See CRS Report R43447, Unlawfully Present Aliens, Higher Education, In-State Tuition, and Financial Aid: Legal Analysis, by Kate M. Manuel.

[109] U.S. Const., art. III, §2, cl. 1.

[110] Baker v. Carr, 369 U.S. 186, 204 (1962).

[111] See, e.g., Lujan v. Defenders of Wildlife, 504 U.S. 555, 560-61 (1992). Additional requirements—involving so-called "prudential standing" could also present issues. These requirements are reflected in the rule that plaintiffs must be "within the 'zone of interests to be protected or regulated by the statute or constitutional guarantee'" that they allege to have been violated in order to be found to have standing. See, e.g., Valley Forge Christian College v. Am. United for Separation of Church and State, 454 U.S. 464 (1982); Assoc. of Data Processing Serv. Orgs. v. Camp, 397 U.S. 150 (1970).

[112] See, e.g., Lance v. Coffman, 549 U.S. 437, 439 (2007) ("A plaintiff raising only a generally available grievance about government—claiming only harm to his and every citizen's interest in [the] proper application of the Constitution and laws, and seeking relief that no more directly [or] tangibly benefits him than it does the public at large—does not state an Article III case or controversy.") (internal quotations omitted)); Lujan v. Defenders of

Wildlife, 504 U.S. 555, 562 (1992) ("[W]hen the plaintiff is not himself the object of the government action or inaction he challenges, standing is not precluded, but is ordinarily 'substantially more difficult' to establish.").

[113] See, e.g., Donelon v. La. Div. of Admin. Law ex rel. Wise, 522 F.3d 564 (5th Cir. 2008) (Louisiana Commissioner of Insurance lacked standing to challenge the constitutionality of a state law which he alleged violated the Constitution); Finch v. Miss. State Med. Ass'n, Inc., 585 F.2d 765, 773-75 (5th Cir. 1978) (governor of Mississippi lacked standing to challenge a state law whose enforcement, he believed, would cause him to violate his oath to uphold the federal and state constitutions).

[114] Compare Drake v. Obama, 664 F.3d 774, 780 (9th Cir. 2011) ("The notion that [the plaintiff] will be disciplined by the military for obeying President Obama's orders is entirely speculative. He might be disciplined for disobeying those orders, but he has an 'available course of action which subjects [him] to no concrete adverse consequences'—he can obey the orders of the Commander-in-Chief.") (emphasis in original)) with Crane, 920 F. Supp. 2d at 738-40 (finding that the ICE agents challenging DACA have "suffered an injury-in-fact by virtue of being compelled to violate a federal statute upon pain of adverse employment action," and otherwise satisfy the requirements for standing).

[115] Crane, 2013 U.S. Dist. LEXIS 187005.

[116] 521 U.S. 811 (1997).

[117] See, e.g., Texas v. United States, 106 F.3d 661, 664 (5th Cir. 1997) ("The [plaintiffs'] amended complaint alleges that hundreds of thousands of undocumented immigrants live in Texas as a direct consequence of federal immigration policy. The State alleges that federal defendants have violated the Constitution and immigration laws by failing to reimburse Texas for its educational, medical, and criminal justice expenditures on undocumented aliens. The State seeks an order enjoining federal defendants from failing to pay for these alleged financial consequences of federal immigration policy and requiring prospective payment as well as restitution for the State's relevant expenditures since 1988. These expenditures are estimated at $1.34 billion for 1993 alone."). Other states also made similar claims in the mid-1990s. See Arizona v. United States, 104 F.3d 1095 (9th Cir. 1997); California v. United States, 104 F.3d 1086 (9th Cir. 1997); New Jersey v. United States, 91 F.3d 463 (3d Cir. 1996); Padavan v. United States, 82 F.3d 23 (2d Cir. 1996); Chiles v. United States, 69 F.3d 1094 (11th Cir. 1995), cert. denied, 517 U.S. 1188 (1996).

[118] See, e.g., Texas, 106 F.3d at 664 (noting that the district court had found the plaintiffs lacked standing); Crane, 920 F. Supp. 2d at 745-46 (finding that Mississippi's "asserted fiscal injury is purely speculative because there is no concrete evidence that the costs associated with the presence of illegal aliens in the state of Mississippi have increased or will increase as a result of the Directive or the Morton Memorandum").

[119] See, e.g., Texas, 106 F.3d at 664 n.2 ("For purposes of today's disposition we assume, without deciding, that the plaintiffs have standing."); Florida, 69 F.3d at 1096 (appellate court noting that the district court did not address the standing issue, and that the appellate court would "suppose" the state has standing to raise its claims).

[120] See, e.g., Texas, 106 F.3d at 665; New Jersey, 91 F.3d at 469; Padavan, 82 F.3d at 27-28; Chiles, 69 F.3d at 1097.

[121] See, e.g., Baker v. Carr, 369 U.S. 186, 217 (1962) ("Prominent on the surface of any case held to involve a political question is found a textually demonstrable constitutional commitment of the issue to a coordinate political department; or a lack of judicially discoverable and manageable standards for resolving it, [among other things].").

[122] See, e.g., Josh Gerstein, White House Readies Immigration Legal Defense, POLITICO, Nov. 19, 2014, available at http://www.politico.com/story/2014/11/barack-obama-executive-order-immigration-113051.html.

[123] Mendoza v. Perez, 754 F.3d 1002, 1011 (D.C. Cir. 2014), rehearing en banc denied, 2014 U.S. App. LEXIS 15437 (Aug. 11, 2014). See also Int'l Union of Bricklayers & Allied Craftsmen v. Meese, 761 F.3d 798 (D.C. Cir. 1985) (finding that plaintiffs had standing where they alleged three instances wherein aliens were admitted under B-1 visas (for temporary business visitors) to "perform work of which the union members are said to be capable").

[124] See generally CRS Report R43223, The Framework for Foreign Workers' Labor Protections Under Federal Law, by Margaret Mikyung Lee and Jon O. Shimabukuro.

[125] Thus, the current situation could potentially be said to resemble earlier litigation in which the plaintiffs alleged improper competition from foreign workers, but were found to lack standing to challenge executive actions not involving employment-based visas whose issuance involves protections for U.S. workers. See, e.g., Programmers Guild v. Chertoff, 338 Fed. App'x 239 (3d Cir. 2009) (finding that the plaintiffs lacked standing to challenge the 17-month extension of OPT because nothing in the INA conditioned the entry of aliens into the United States on an F-1 visa "on noninterference with domestic labor conditions"), cert. denied sub nom. Guild v. Napolitano, 559 U.S. 1067 (2010); Fed. for Am. Immigr. Reform, Inc. v. Reno, 93 F.3d 897, 899 (D.C. Cir. 1996) (finding that the plaintiffs lacked standing to challenge the Executive's paroling of Cuban nationals into the United States because the INA imposes no employment-related restrictions upon the parole of aliens into the United States).

[126] Compare Drew Desilver, Executive Actions on Immigration Have a Long History, Pew Research Center, Nov. 21, 2014, available at http://www.pewresearch.org/fact-tank/2014/11/21/executive-actions-on-immigration-have-longhistory/ with David Frum, Reagan and Bush Offer No Precedent for Obama's Amnesty Order, THE ATLANTIC, Nov. 18, 2014, available at http://www.theatlantic.com/politics/archive/2014/11/the-weak-argument-defending-executiveamnesty/382906/.

[127] See Zachary S. Price, Enforcement Discretion and Executive Duty, 67 VAND. L. REV. 671, 675 (2004) (prosecutorial discretion not extending to "entire categories" of aliens); Dream On, supra note 4, at 846 (similar).

[128] See Refugee Resettlement Act of 1960, P.L. 86-648, §1, 74 Stat. 504 (July 14, 1960) (providing that, "under the terms of section 212(d)(5) of the Immigration and Nationality Act[,] the Attorney General may parole into the United States, pursuant to such regulations as he may prescribe, an alien refugee-escapee," subject to certain conditions).

[129] See, e.g., Department of State Authorization Act, FY1984-1985, P.L. 98-164, §1012, 97 Stat. 1062 (Nov. 22, 1983) (expressing the "sense of the Congress" that the Executive ought to consider persons from El Salvador for EVD).

[130] But see Glenn Kessler, Obama's Claim that George H.W. Bush Gave Relief to "40 percent" of Undocumented Immigrants, Wash. Post, Nov. 24, 2014, available at http://www.washingtonpost.com/blogs/fact-checker/wp/2014/11/ 24/did-george-h-w-bush-really-shield-1-5-million-illegal-immigrants-nope/.

[131] See 1990 Family Fairness memorandum, supra note 48; INS, Office of the Commissioner, Family Fairness: Guidelines for Voluntary Departures under 8 C.F.R. 242.5 for the Ineligible Spouses and Children of Legalized Aliens, Nov. 1987 (copy on file with the author).

[132] See, e.g., IMMIGRATION REFORM AND CONTROL ACT OF 1986 OVERSIGHT: HEARINGS BEFORE THE SUBCOMMITTEE ON IMMIGRATION, REFUGEES, AND INTERNATIONAL LAW OF THE COMMITTEE ON THE JUDICIARY, HOUSE OF REPRESENTATIVES, 101ST CONG., 1ST SESS., May 10 & 17, 1989, at 48 (noting that some spouses and children of legalized aliens who applied for relief were "issues Orders to Show Cause ..., which initiate deportation proceedings").

[133] DHS has left open the possibility that aliens who apply, but are ineligible for, relief through DACA could be subject to immigration enforcement actions. See Frequently Asked Questions, supra note 13 ("Information provided in this request is protected from disclosure ... for the purpose of immigration enforcement proceedings unless the requestor meets the criteria for the issuance of a Notice To Appear or a referral to ICE under the criteria set forth in USCIS' Notice to Appear guidance.") However, it is unclear whether any such actions have been taken.

[134] Both of the Family Fairness initiatives were adopted after the Immigration Reform and Control Act (IRCA) of 1986, P.L. 99-603, 100 Stat. 3359 (Nov. 6, 1986), was enacted, and both preceded the Immigration Act of 1990, P.L. 101- 649, 104 Stat. 4978 (Nov. 29, 1990).

In: Presidential Executive Action on Immigration ISBN: 978-1-63482-263-3
Editor: David Ferguson

Chapter 3

THE PRESIDENT'S IMMIGRATION ACCOUNTABILITY EXECUTIVE ACTION OF NOVEMBER 20, 2014: OVERVIEW AND ISSUES*

William A. Kandel, Jerome P. Bjelopera, Andorra Bruno and Alison Siskin

SUMMARY

On November 20, 2014, President Obama announced his Immigration Accountability Executive Action which revises some U.S. immigration policies and initiates several programs, including a revised border security policy for the Southwest border; deferred action programs for some unauthorized aliens; revised interior enforcement priorities; changes to aid the entry of skilled workers; the promotion of immigrant integration and naturalization; and several other initiatives the President indicated would improve the U.S. immigration system. The most controversial among these provisions will grant deferred action to as many as 5 million unauthorized aliens.

* This is an edited, reformatted and augmented version of a Congressional Research Service publication R43852, prepared for Members and Committees of Congress dated January 8, 2015.

The President announced the executive actions through ten Department of Homeland Security (DHS) memoranda, two White House memoranda, and three Department of Labor (DOL) fact sheets. Together, they comprise the following initiatives:

- ***Border Security*:** forming three new task forces as part of DHS's Southern Border and Approaches Campaign Strategy that integrates efforts not only *within* DHS's Customs and Border Protection (CBP) but also among other DHS agencies, such as Immigration and Customs Enforcement (ICE), U.S. Citizenship and Immigration Services (USCIS), and the U.S. Coast Guard;
- ***Interior Enforcement and Removals*:** revising priorities for immigration enforcement and detention; ending the Secure Communities program and replacing it with the Priority Enforcement Program (PEP), collecting and disseminating improved metrics on removals, and reforming the employment structure for ICE Enforcement and Removal Office (ERO) agents;
- ***Expanded Deferred Action for Childhood Arrivals (DACA)*:** increasing the population eligible for the DACA program by expanding the eligibility criteria, and extending the duration of DACA and its related work authorization from two to three years;
- ***Deferred Action for Parents of Americans and Lawful Permanent Residents (DAPA)*:** allowing parents of U.S. citizens and lawful permanent residents (LPRs) to request deferred action and employment authorization if they meet residency and other criteria and pass required background checks;
- ***Parole Rules*:** revising conditions under which eligible family members of military personnel, persons traveling abroad, and certain entrepreneurs may receive parole;
- ***Provisional Unlawful Presence Waivers*:** expanding the use of provisional unlawful presence waivers beyond spouses and minor children of U.S. citizens to also include the spouses and minor children of LPRs as well as the adult children of U.S. citizens, and clarifying the "extreme hardship" standard that must be met to obtain this waiver;
- ***High Skilled Workers*:** ensuring that all statutorily available LPR visas are fully utilized, reviewing the labor certification program and its regulations to strengthen its integrity and responsiveness to workforce changes, providing foreign workers with greater flexibility

to change jobs, expanding the use of national interest waivers to retain selected highly qualified workers, expanding opportunities for students to gain on-the-job training through administrative rule changes, and clarifying the meaning of "specialized knowledge" to ensure U.S. workers are not being unfairly displaced;

- ***Immigrant Integration and Naturalization*:** initiating an inter-agency task force to identify and promote both immigrant integration "best practices" within states and localities as well as facilitating steps that can be taken administratively within and among federal agencies, and encouraging eligible LPRs to naturalize through additional payment options and possible partial fee waivers;
- ***Immigrant Visa System*:** providing recommendations to streamline, modernize, and improve immigrant and nonimmigrant visa processing;
- ***Labor Protection*:** creating an inter-agency working group to promote effective and consistent enforcement of federal labor, employment, and immigration laws to protect all workers regardless of legal status; and
- ***Crime Victims*:** expanding the DOL Wage and Hour Division's role in supporting foreign national victims of human trafficking and other select crimes.

According to the President, the actions were taken in response to the absence of legislation addressing major problems within the immigration system. The President has stated that his actions are temporary, and that his successor can rescind them. Those opposed to the executive actions argue they were taken largely for political purposes. They contend that once granted, such temporary measures would be difficult to revoke. Separately, a debate has arisen as to whether the President has the legal authority to take such actions, with the Administration and others arguing the President's actions fall within his authority, and many in Congress arguing the President has overstepped it. That debate and its attendant legal questions are beyond the scope of this report.

Because the President announced his executive actions relatively recently, little guidance is available to clarify policies and answer questions related to the revisions and initiatives they include. The two deferred action programs, both of which require petitioners to submit fees, are the only initiatives in the executive action supported by independent fee-supported funding. The rest rely largely on changes in rules and regulations and on the coordination and marshaling of existing administrative resources. As the Administration proceeds to implement the executive actions, some in Congress have vowed to halt some or all of them.

INTRODUCTION

On November 20, 2014, President Obama announced his Immigration Accountability Executive Action which revises some U.S. immigration policies and initiates several programs, including a revised border security policy for the Southwest border; deferred action programs for some unauthorized aliens; revised interior enforcement priorities; changes to aid the entry of skilled workers; the promotion of immigrant integration and naturalization; and several other initiatives the President indicated would improve the U.S. immigration system. The most controversial among these provisions will grant deferred action to as many as 5 million unauthorized aliens.[1] The President announced the executive action through ten Department of Homeland Security (DHS) memoranda, two White House memoranda, and three Department of Labor (DOL) fact sheets.

According to the President, the actions were taken in response to the absence of legislation addressing major problems within the immigration system. The President has stated that his actions are temporary, and that his successor can rescind them. Those opposed to the executive actions argue they were taken largely for political purposes. They contend that once granted, such temporary measures would be difficult to revoke. Separately, a debate has arisen as to whether the President has the legal authority to take such actions, with the Administration and others arguing the President's actions fall within his authority, and many in Congress arguing the President has overstepped it.[2] That debate and its attendant legal questions are beyond the scope of this report. As the Administration proceeds to implement the executive actions, some in Congress have vowed to halt some or all of them.

Overview of Major U.S. Immigration Policy Issues

Policy makers and immigration observers widely agree that the U.S. immigration system is "broken," but they disagree on measures to fix it. Underlying these different views are broader and more fundamental debates about how many temporary and permanent immigrants should be admitted into the United States, how those immigrants should be selected for admission (e.g., needed skills, relationship to U.S. residents), and the funding levels and appropriate mix of immigration enforcement measures, among other issues.[3]

Long-standing immigration-related challenges include: an estimated population of over 10 million unauthorized individuals, a large portion of whom have lived in the country for over a decade and have U.S. citizen and lawful permanent resident (LPR) children;[4] increasing competition among more advanced nations for the "best and brightest" workers, including U.S. educated science, technology, engineering, and mathematics (STEM) graduates;[5] a queue of 4.4 million individuals whose petitions for lawful permanent resident (LPR) status have been approved and who must wait, in some cases decades, for a numerically limited visa to immigrate;[6] and ongoing border security and interior enforcement challenges.[7]

Broad Elements of Immigration Reform

For several years, some Members of Congress have favored "comprehensive immigration reform" (CIR), a label that commonly refers to omnibus legislation that includes increased border security and immigration enforcement, expanded employment eligibility verification, revision of nonimmigrant visas and legal permanent immigration, and legalization for some unauthorized aliens residing in the country. The omnibus legislative approach contrasts with incremental revisions of the Immigration and Nationality Act (INA) and other immigration laws that would address some but not all of these elements, and with sequential reforms that would tackle border security and interior enforcement provisions prior to revising legal immigration or enacting legalization pathways for the unauthorized population residing in the United States.

In 2013, the Senate passed the Border Security, Economic Opportunity, and Immigration Modernization Act (S. 744), a comprehensive immigration reform bill. S. 744 contained provisions that, among other things, would have increased border security and interior enforcement, expanded employment eligibility verification and worksite enforcement, offered a conditional path to legal status for many unauthorized aliens, reformed permanent immigrant and temporary nonimmigrant visas, and revised humanitarian admissions. The House took a different approach to immigration reform. Rather than consider a single comprehensive bill, the House acted on separate bills that, among other provisions, would have increased border security and interior enforcement, expanded employment eligibility verification and worksite enforcement, and substantially revised nonimmigrant and immigrant visas.[8]

Summary of the President's Executive Action

The President's "Immigration Accountability Executive Action," announced on November 20, 2014, includes initiatives covering the following policy areas:

- border security;
- interior enforcement and removals;
- Deferred Action for Childhood Arrivals (DACA);
- Deferred Action for Parents of Americans and Lawful Permanent Residents (DAPA);
- parole;
- provisional unlawful presence waivers;
- high-skilled foreign workers;
- immigrant integration and naturalization;
- immigrant visa system;
- labor protection; and
- crime victims.

This report reviews each component of the President's executive action based on currently available information. The report is broken out by broad policy areas. Each section begins with a discussion of the context of existing policy, describes the related executive action, and summarizes how the action addresses current immigration policy challenges.

BORDER SECURITY

Security along U.S. borders has been an ongoing subject of congressional interest since the 1970s, when illegal immigration emerged as a serious national problem. The terrorist attacks of September 11, 2001 (9/11) spurred concerns about border security, a core part of DHS's effort to control unauthorized migration. The United States Border Patrol (USBP, Border

Patrol) spearheads this effort as the lead agency along most of the borders. The USBP focuses on the regions between ports of entry (POEs).[9]

In addition to Border Patrol agents, other law enforcement personnel work in U.S. border regions. These include Customs and Border Protection (CBP) officers at POEs; Immigration and Customs Enforcement (ICE) agents; U.S. Coast Guard (USCG) personnel; additional federal law enforcement officers from agencies such as the Drug Enforcement Administration, U.S. Marshals Service, and Department of Agriculture; state and local police; and on occasion, the National Guard. Complementing this array of personnel are CBP's land-based surveillance assets,[10] air and marine surveillance assets,[11] and fencing and physical infrastructure.[12]

USBP has experienced large-scale growth since 2004, and DHS Secretary Johnson and the Obama Administration have argued that the Southwest border is more secure than ever.[13] Yet, some Members of Congress and others have called on the Administration to do more to secure the border. Border security has been a recurrent theme in Congress's debate about comprehensive immigration reform since 2005, and some Members have argued that Congress should not consider additional immigration reforms until the border is more secure.[14]

USBP is responsible for enforcing U.S. immigration law and other federal laws along the border and for preventing all unlawful entries into the United States, including entries of terrorists, unauthorized aliens, weapons of mass destruction, illicit narcotics, and other contraband. In discharging its duties, USBP patrols roughly 7,500 miles of U.S. international borders with Mexico and Canada and the coastal waters around Florida and Puerto Rico.

Along the border, USBP's staffing has grown from 9,511 in FY2004 to 18,611 in FY2013, with a slight dip to 18,127 in FY2014 (**Figure 1**). At the same time, apprehensions at the Southwest border have declined with an uptick in recent years partly due to a rise in the number of unaccompanied children crossing illegally. It is unclear how the expansion in USBP personnel has influenced unlawful migration, but the Obama Administration and DHS Secretary Johnson have touted these two numbers as indicative of improved security along the Southwest border.[15]

In recent years, CBP and USBP have developed border security plans. In May 2012, CBP released the most recent iteration, the "2012-2016 Border Patrol Strategic Plan." It shifts attention from resource acquisition and deployment to the strategic allocation of resources by "focusing enhanced capabilities against the highest threats and rapidly responding along the border."[16] From an operational perspective, this plan emphasizes the collection and analysis of information about evolving border threats; integration of Border Patrol and CBP planning across different border sectors and among the full range of federal, state, local, tribal, and international organizations involved in border security; and rapid Border Patrol response to specific border threats.[17]

Coordinating Border Security

In one project to enhance the coordination of complex border security and inspection efforts, CBP developed the Arizona Joint Field Command (JFC). The JFC emerged in 2011 as "an organizational realignment" bringing together the Border Patrol with CBP's other key components,[18] "under a unified command structure to integrate CBP's border security, commercial enforcement, and trade facilitation missions to more effectively meet the unique challenges faced in the Arizona area of operations."[19] The JFC includes more than 6,700 CBP employees and covers the entire state of Arizona and parts of California.

FY2004-FY2014

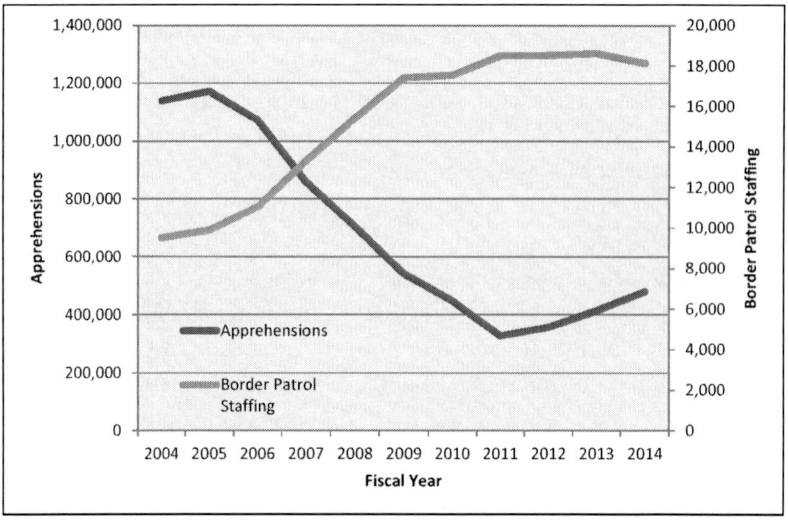

Source: Jeh Charles Johnson, DHS Secretary, "Border Security in the 21st Century," slides from presentation delivered at the Center for Strategic and International Studies, Washington, DC, October 9, 2014.

Figure 1. Apprehensions and Border Patrol Staffing along the Southwest Border.

DHS has announced coordination measures that appear to go much further than the JFC. Secretary Johnson first revealed the development of such border-security plans in May 2014. In written congressional testimony he describes a "Southern Border and Approaches Campaign" planning effort devised to create

> a strategic framework to further enhance security of our Southern border. Plan development will be guided by specific outcomes and quantifiable targets for border security, approved by me, and will address improved information sharing, continued enhancement and integration of sensors, and unified command and control structures as appropriate. The overall planning effort will also include a subset of campaign plans focused on addressing challenges within specific geographic areas.[20]

Discussion

On November 20, 2014, DHS Secretary Johnson expanded on the campaign by "commissioning" three Joint Task Forces.[21] Unlike the Arizona JFC, which brings together elements *within* CBP, the three Joint Task Forces will bring together personnel from CBP as well as *other* DHS agencies—the U.S. Coast Guard, Immigration and Customs Enforcement, and U.S. Citizenship and Immigration Services (USCIS). The Joint Task Forces will also "integrate capabilities of the remaining [DHS] components as needed." According to Secretary Johnson, "two of these task forces will be geographically based and one will be functionally focused." Joint Task Force East will cover "the Southern maritime border and approaches." Joint Task Force West will have responsibility for the southern land border and the West Coast, while an entity dubbed Joint Task Force Investigations "will focus on investigations in support of the geographic Task Forces." The memo lays out broad missions and objectives and sets a 90 day timeframe to "realign personnel and stand up headquarters capabilities within each Joint Task Force."

Thus far, more details about the Joint Task Forces are scarce, and several key questions loom:

- Will DHS alter its command and control structures—as well as those of its component agencies—to accommodate these new bodies?

- What authority will each Joint Task Force leader[22] have over Task Force personnel, immediate priorities, and budgets? Will such authority supersede the authority of component leadership in DHS?
- What metrics will be used to assess the effectiveness of the Joint Task Forces?
- How will jurisdictional disputes between Joint Task Forces and issues related to competing mission priorities be settled?

ENFORCEMENT PRIORITIES, SECURE COMMUNITIES, AND PAY REFORM

Since its enactment in 1952, the Immigration and Nationality Act has given the Attorney General and more recently the DHS Secretary discretion to exercise the power to remove foreign nationals. Since at least 1975, a series of policy memorandums published by the former Immigration and Naturalization Service (INS) and DHS has provided guidance to immigration officers who institute removal proceedings against an alien. The guidance noted which categories of foreign nationals to prioritize for removal (i.e., prosecutorial discretion).[23]

ICE Enforcement and Removal Operations (ERO) is chiefly responsible for locating removable aliens, managing custody of aliens undergoing removal procedures, and ensuring that aliens directed to depart from the United States do so (either by witnessing their removals or by physically removing the aliens). In addition, certain other DHS personnel may initiate a removal process against an alien.[24]

On November 20, 2014, the DHS Secretary announced new department-wide policies for enforcement priorities and the apprehension, detention, and removal of aliens.[25] This guidance is effective on January 5, 2015. In addition, Secretary Johnson announced a review and actions to overhaul the pay scale for immigration officers in ERO.[26]

Enforcement Priorities

Secretary Johnson wrote in the November 20, 2014 memorandum on enforcement priorities:

> Due to limited resources, DHS and its components cannot respond to all immigration violations or remove all persons illegally in the United States. As is true of virtually every other law enforcement agency, DHS must exercise prosecutorial discretion in the enforcement of the law. And, in the exercise of that discretion, DHS can and should develop smart enforcement priorities, and ensure that use of its limited resources is devoted to the pursuit of those priorities.[27]

The memorandum states that prosecutorial discretion should apply to initiating or suspending a removal proceeding as well as other enforcement decisions, such as deciding who to stop, question, arrest and detain; whether to continue to pursue a removal case; and whether to grant deferred action, parole, or a stay of removal. While DHS may exercise prosecutorial discretion at any stage of an enforcement proceeding, the policy states it is preferable to do so as early as possible to conserve government resources.

The memorandum lays out the following enforcement priorities:

- *(Highest) Priority 1: threats to national security, border security, and public safety*
  - aliens engaged in or suspected of terrorism or espionage, or who otherwise pose a threat to national security;
  - aliens apprehended at the border or ports of entry while attempting to unlawfully enter the United States;
  - aliens convicted of an offense that involves participating in a criminal street gang,[28] or aliens who are 16 years or older who intentionally participated in an organized criminal gang to further illegal activity of the gang; and
  - aliens convicted of felonies.[29]
- *Priority 2: misdemeanants and new immigration violators*
  - aliens convicted of three or more misdemeanors[30] or a "significant misdemeanor;"[31]
  - aliens who are unlawfully present and were not physically present before January 1, 2014; and
  - aliens who have significantly abused the "visa or visa waiver programs" (i.e., terms of admittance).
- *Priority 3: aliens issued final orders of removal after December 31, 2013.*

According to the memorandum, unless certain circumstances are met, aliens described in *Priority 1* must be prioritized for removal, those in Priority 2 should be removed, and those in *Priority 3* should generally be removed.[32]

The President's executive action issued on November 20, 2014, revises enforcement priorities and rescinds and supersedes related policies issued in 2011 and 2012 by then-ICE Director John Morton.[33] The previous priority levels were (1) aliens who pose a danger to national security or a risk to public safety; (2) recent entrants; and (3) aliens with final orders of removal (i.e., fugitives or absconders) or who otherwise obstruct immigration controls. The most substantive change in enforcement priorities between the newly issued policy and policies from earlier years[34] is that an alien who was issued a final order of removal prior to 2014 is no longer an enforcement priority, provided he or she is neither a criminal nor a national security concern.[35] Other changes include increasing the priority level of aliens apprehended at or between ports of entry while attempting to illegally enter the country, and providing more specificity on the types of misdemeanor offenses that make an alien a focus for removal.

Detention Priorities

As with the previous Morton policy memorandum on detention and removal priorities,[36] the November 20, 2014, memorandum on enforcement priorities specifies that as a general rule, detention resources should be used to support enforcement priorities noted above or for aliens subject to mandatory detention under the law.[37] In keeping with earlier policy, the memorandum also states that, absent extraordinary circumstances or the statutory requirement of mandatory detention, ICE should not detain aliens who are

- known to be suffering from serious physical or mental illness;
- disabled, elderly, pregnant, or nursing;
- primary caretakers of children or infirm persons; or
- not in the public interest to detain.

Removal Statistics

ICE and the Office of Immigration Statistics (OIS) both report removal statistics, but immigration observers have raised questions about their accuracy.[38] In addition, removal statistics are used to evaluate DHS's adherence to stated policies on enforcement priorities.[39] Through the executive action, DHS Secretary Johnson directs OIS, with the cooperation of CBP, ICE, and USCIS, to create the capability to collect and maintain data reflecting the numbers of those apprehended, removed, returned, or otherwise repatriated by any component of DHS. He further directs that these statistics be made publically available on an annual basis.

Secure Communities/Interoperability

Secure Communities was the original name given to an information sharing program that uses biometric data to screen for removable aliens as people are being booked into jails. The program began in late 2008 in about a dozen jurisdictions and since FY2013 has been operational in all state and local law enforcement jurisdictions in the country. As early as 2011, DHS began referring to this program as *interoperability* between local law enforcement, the Federal Bureau of Investigation (FBI), and DHS.[40]

Secure Communities/interoperability is not an enforcement unit. When law enforcement agencies book (take custody of) someone and submit the person's fingerprints to the FBI for criminal background checks,[41] the fingerprints are also automatically checked against DHS's Automated Biometric Identification System (IDENT) database.[42] If the person is matched to an immigration record in IDENT, ICE is notified and determines whether any action is necessary or appropriate based on the agency's enforcement priorities.[43] Aliens identified for removal are placed in removal proceedings by ICE agents, typically from the Criminal Alien program (CAP).[44]

As part of the President's executive action, Secretary Johnson directs ICE to discontinue Secure Communities.[45] However, the data interoperability between DOJ and DHS created under the name Secure Communities is not being discontinued. Instead, the program is being renamed and enforcement priorities changed for those identified as possibly removable aliens through the interoperability process. Consistent with the policy memorandum on enforcement priorities, the policy memorandum on Secure Communities specifies that ICE should only seek a transfer for an alien in state or local custody if he or she has been convicted of a *Priority 1* offense or of multiple or significant misdemeanors. Under the revised priorities, unless aliens pose a demonstrable risk to national security, enforcement actions will only be taken against those convicted of specifically enumerated crimes. The new program will be called the Priority Enforcement Program (PEP).

The Secure Communities memorandum also addresses the issue of "immigration detainers." These are documents in which ICE advises law enforcement agencies of its interest in individuals whom these agencies are detaining, and to take actions (such as holding the alien temporarily) to facilitate their removal.[46] The increased use of immigration detainers under Secure Communities has raised legal questions regarding their use.[47] Under the revised policy, ICE will replace requests for detention with requests for notification (i.e., that state or local law enforcement notify ICE of an alien's pending release from custody). Under special circumstances, a detention request may be issued if the person is subject to a final order of removal or if sufficient probable cause exists to find the person removable.

Some contend that the Secure Communities program has led to unfair treatment of selected individuals (e.g., a person is arrested rather than just given a warning or ticket because of his or her perceived immigration status) as well as some improper arrests and unlawful detention (e.g., a person is arrested on a false change because he or she is perceived to be unlawfully present).[48] In the Secure Communities memorandum of November 20, 2014, the DHS Secretary directs the Office of Civil Rights and Civil Liberties to develop and implement a plan to monitor state and local law enforcement agencies participating in the transfer of foreign nationals to ICE.

Personnel Reform

As part of the President's executive action, DHS also announced a recalibration of the workforce and pay structure for ICE Enforcement and Removal Operations (ERO) personnel."[49] The related memorandum directs ERO and the DHS Office of the Chief Human Capital Officer to review the job series and premium pay coverage for ERO officers and determine any changes that may be required. The Administration will then pursue and prioritize regulations and legislation necessary to achieve the desired changes. According to the Administration, ERO's enforcement strategy and initiatives have shifted toward investigations, identification, location, arrest, prosecution, and removal of criminal aliens and other aliens who pose risks to national security. However, ERO's personnel structure lags behind other law enforcement agencies and other components of ICE, harming morale and presenting management challenges.[50] Some observers contend that personnel issues related to pay structure have existed for years at ERO, and that the reforms within the President's executive actions were timed for political purposes.[51]

Discussion

Since 2002, DHS has made concerted efforts to locate and remove absconders.[52] The President's executive action of November 20, 2014 no longer makes such aliens enforcement priorities if they were issued final orders of removal prior to 2014 and are neither criminals nor national security concerns. At the start of FY2014, ICE reported a backlog of 469,151 fugitive aliens who had not been apprehended.[53] The Administration stated it is undertaking this policy to allow DHS to focus its limited resources on higher enforcement priorities. It is not known, however, how many fugitive aliens would qualify for the President's deferred action initiatives, but some overlap between the two programs can be expected. Time will be required to measure the impact of the new enforcement priorities on the types of aliens who are located and removed.

In addition, until implemented it remains unclear exactly what the effect of the new PEP program will be, compared to the former and in some ways comparable Secure Communities program it replaced. The enforcement priorities memorandum of November 20, 2014, suggests that ICE will issue fewer detainers with state and local law enforcement, focusing only on higher priority cases. It is also unclear how well the new requests for notification will effectuate the transfer of aliens to ICE custody, given that not all jurisdictions currently accept ICE requests for detention.

Deferred Action, Parole, and Provisional Inadmissibility Waivers

How to address the unauthorized alien[54] population in the United States has arguably been the most divisive issue in recent discussions about immigration reform. Proposals to enable unauthorized aliens to become U.S. lawful permanent residents (LPRs) have been key flash points in the congressional debate. Various legalization proposals have been introduced in recent Congresses, but none have been enacted. One key difference among these proposals has been their scope. Some bills have been targeted at particular segments of the unauthorized population. For example, legislation known as the Development, Relief, and Education for Alien Minors (DREAM) Act has proposed to enable certain unauthorized aliens who arrived in the United States as children to obtain LPR status through a two-stage process.[55] Other more controversial measures, such as the major Senate immigration reform bill considered in the 113th Congress,[56] have aimed to provide LPR status more broadly.

While only legislative action can bestow legal immigration status, the Obama Administration has used other mechanisms to enable unauthorized aliens to remain in the United States. The Administration has also taken steps to address the impact of provisions in the Immigration and Nationality Act (INA) that make aliens who have been unlawfully present in the United States for more than 180 days and then depart, inadmissible to the country for a specified period of time. These provisions are known as the 3- and 10-year bars. Through a recent set of executive actions, the Obama Administration is providing eligibility for two forms of temporary immigration relief—deferred action and parole—for certain segments of the unauthorized population, as well as expanding the availability of certain types of waivers of the unlawful presence grounds of inadmissibility in the INA.[57]

Deferred Action

DHS defines deferred action as "a discretionary determination to defer removal action of an individual as an act of prosecutorial discretion."[58] In 2012, in the absence of congressional action on DREAM Act legislation, DHS issued a memorandum announcing that certain unauthorized individuals who were brought to the United States as children and meet other criteria would be considered on a case-by-case basis for deferred action for two years, subject to renewal.[59] The eligibility criteria established for this initiative, known as deferred action for childhood arrivals, or DACA, were similar to those for relief in DREAM Act bills. Among the DACA criteria were (1) being under age 16 at time of entry into the United States; (2) residing continuously in the United States since June 15, 2007; and (3) being below age 31 on June 15, 2012. The DACA initiative is administered by DHS's U.S. Citizenship and Immigration Services (USCIS). Aliens apply for employment authorization at the same time that they submit their applications for consideration of DACA.[60]

On November 20, 2014, DHS Secretary Johnson announced an expansion of the original DACA initiative and the establishment of another DACA-like process to exercise prosecutorial discretion for another subgroup of unauthorized aliens in the United States.[61]

Expansion of Eligibility for DACA

The 2014 DHS memorandum on prosecutorial discretion directs USCIS to make specified changes to the DACA initiative that expand the pool of potential beneficiaries, as follows:

- elimination of the "below age 31 on June 15, 2012" requirement;
- advancement of the required starting date of continuous residence from June 15, 2007, to January 1, 2010; and
- extension of the initial grant and renewal periods for DACA and accompanying employment authorization from two to three years.

In the memorandum, DHS directs USCIS to begin accepting applications under the expanded DACA parameters in 90 days.

Establishment of the New Deferred Action Process

In the memorandum, the DHS Secretary further directs USCIS to establish a DACA-like process for exercising prosecutorial discretion toward another group of unauthorized individuals—parents of U.S. citizens or LPRs—who meet specified criteria. In addition to not having a lawful immigration status on November 20, 2014, a potential beneficiary must:

- be the parent of a U.S. citizen or LPR;
- have resided continuously in the United States since before January 1, 2010;
- be physically present in the United States on November 20, 2014, and at the time of making a request for consideration of deferred action with USCIS;
- not be an enforcement priority; and
- not present any other factors that make the grant of deferred action inappropriate.

The memorandum specifies that, as under DACA, applicants will apply for employment authorization at the same time that they submit their applications for consideration of deferred action. Grants of deferred action and accompanying work authorization under this process will be valid for a three-year period. In the memorandum, the DHS Secretary directs USCIS to begin accepting applications under the new deferred action process within 180 days.

Deferred action is also addressed in another DHS memorandum where the DHS Secretary directs USCIS to consider granting deferred action to unauthorized family members of U.S. military service members and veterans who are not eligible for parole-in-place (see "Parole").[62]

Parole

The INA authorizes the DHS Secretary to "parole into the United States temporarily under such conditions as he may prescribe only on a case-by-case basis for urgent humanitarian reasons or significant public benefit any alien applying for admission into the United States."[63] Parole does not constitute formal admission to the United States; an individual granted parole is still considered an applicant for admission. Although parole is used most often to allow an alien who is outside the United States to enter the country, it also has been granted to unauthorized aliens who are physically present in the United States but who have never been lawfully admitted.[64] Parole granted to those present in the United States is known as *parole-in-place*. Another procedure, advance parole, may be authorized by USCIS to enable an alien in the United States to travel abroad and, upon return, be considered for parole.

Expansion of Use of Parole-in-Place for Military Families

Ongoing DHS policy makes certain family members of U.S military service members and veterans eligible for parole-in-place. Covered family members are spouses, children, and parents of active duty members—and former members—of the U.S. Armed Forces and the Selected Reserve of the Ready Reserve.[65] In his November 20, 2014 memorandum, the DHS Secretary reports that the Department of Defense (DOD) has requested that DHS expand the application of its military parole-in-place policy to cover family members of U.S. citizens and LPRs who seek to enlist in the U.S. Armed Forces.[66] In the memorandum, the Secretary directs USCIS to issue new policies on the use of parole-in-place for certain spouses, children, and parents of U.S. citizens and LPRs seeking to enlist.

Advance Parole

The November 20, 2014, DHS memorandum *Directive to Provide Consistency Regarding Advance Parole* addresses a Board of Immigration Appeals (BIA)[67] decision concerning advance parole and one of the grounds of inadmissibility in the INA related to unlawful presence.[68] In the *Matter of Arrabally*, the BIA decided that "individuals who travel abroad after a grant of advance parole do not effectuate a 'departure . . . from the United States' within the meaning of [INA] section 212(a)(9)(B)(i)."[69] Under INA §212(a)(9)(B)(i)(1), an alien who has been unlawfully present in the United States for more than 180 days but less than one year, voluntarily departs, and seeks admission within three years is inadmissible (3-year bar); and under INA §212(a)(9)(B)(i) (2), an alien who has been unlawfully present in the United States for one year or more and seeks admission within 10 years of such alien's departure or removal date is inadmissible (10-year bar). If, in accordance with the *Arabally* decision, travel on advance parole does not constitute a departure, then the 3- and 10-year bars on admissibility would not be triggered in such cases. In the DHS memorandum, the DHS Secretary provides notice that he has asked the DHS General Counsel to issue legal guidance clarifying that "in all cases when an individual physically leaves the United States pursuant to a grant of advance parole, that individual shall not have made a 'departure' within the meaning of section 212(a)(9)(B)(i) of the INA."

Provisional Unlawful Presence Waivers

The INA provides for specified family members of U.S. citizens or LPRs and specified categories of workers to be admitted to the United States for permanent residence as LPRs. The process of becoming an LPR through either the family-based or employment-based route has multiple steps.[70] In most cases, the sponsoring family member or employer must file an immigrant visa petition on behalf of the alien with USCIS.[71] Among the general requirements for obtaining a visa or gaining lawful admission to the United States is that an individual must be admissible to the country. In other words, the individual cannot be inadmissible under the enumerated grounds of inadmissibility in the INA (see "Advance Parole"). Some grounds of inadmissibility are subject to exceptions and waivers.

Unauthorized aliens in the United States with approved immigrant visa petitions may face difficulties in obtaining LPR status. The process of becoming an LPR from within the United States is known as *adjustment of status*. The main adjustment of status provision in the INA[72] applies to aliens who have been inspected and admitted, or paroled, into the United States or who qualify for classification under the Violence Against Women Act (VAWA) and who meet other specified requirements. These requirements include that (1) the alien is the beneficiary of an approved immigrant visa petition; (2) an immigrant visa is immediately available;[73] and (3) the alien is admissible to the United States. Except for VAWA cases, unauthorized aliens who entered the United States without inspection are ineligible to adjust to LPR status under the main INA adjustment of status provision. Unauthorized aliens who initially were admitted or paroled into the country are generally ineligible to adjust status unless they qualify for an exception.[74]

The alternative to adjusting status in the United States is for the alien to travel to his or her home country to apply for a visa at a U.S. embassy or consulate once a visa number becomes immediately available. If a visa is issued, the alien can use it to gain lawful admission to the United States as an LPR. If, however, an unauthorized alien returns home to apply for a visa, the Department of State (DOS) consular officer who is considering the visa application may find that the alien is inadmissible to the United States for 3 or 10 years based on the alien's prior unlawful presence in the United States, and thereby ineligible for a visa (see "Advance Parole").

A prospective immigrant who is found to be ineligible for a visa by DOS based on his or her prior unlawful presence may be eligible for a waiver. Under INA §212(a)(9)(B)(v), DHS has discretionary authority to grant an alien a waiver if the alien is the spouse or son or daughter of a U.S. citizen or LPR, and it is established that refusal of admission to the alien would result in extreme hardship to the citizen or LPR spouse or parent. Until recently, an alien had to wait until he or she received an ineligibility finding from DOS during the overseas immigrant visa process before applying for a waiver, if eligible.

In 2013, USCIS issued a new rule that made changes to the unlawful presence waiver application process for certain spouses and minor children of U.S. citizens by establishing a provisional unlawful presence waiver. Under the rule, a beneficiary of an approved immigrant visa petition can apply for and receive a provisional waiver of the unlawful presence ground of inadmissibility while still in the United States, if the alien meets all the applicable requirements, including demonstrating that a U.S. citizen spouse or parent would experience extreme hardship if the alien were denied admission to the United States. A recipient of a provisional waiver can then depart the

United States to attend an immigrant visa interview with a DOS consular officer abroad. If the consular officer determines that the applicant, given the approved waiver, is admissible to the United States and eligible for a visa, the officer may issue the immigrant visa, which the individual can present at a port-of-entry to gain lawful admission to the United States.

Expansion of Eligibility for Provisional Unlawful Presence Waivers

As noted, DHS has statutory discretionary authority to grant an unlawful presence waiver to an alien who is the spouse or son or daughter of a U.S. citizen or LPR. Under current regulations, however, eligibility for a provisional waiver is limited to spouses and minor children of U.S. citizens. As part of the President's executive action, the DHS Secretary directs USCIS to expand eligibility for provisional unlawful presence waivers to all statutorily eligible groups for whom an immigrant visa is immediately available.[75] The additional classes to be covered are adult children of U.S. citizens; and spouses, minor children, and adult children of LPRs.

Clarification of Extreme Hardship Standard

In order to receive an unlawful presence waiver under INA §212(a)(9)(B)(v), an applicant must demonstrate that refusing to admit him or her to the United States would result in extreme hardship to a citizen or LPR spouse or parent. The term *extreme hardship* is not defined in the INA. In the *Expansion of the Provisional Waiver Program* memorandum, the DHS Secretary directs USCIS to clarify the factors it considers in making a determination about extreme hardship and "to consider criteria by which a presumption of extreme hardship may be determined to exist."

Discussion

This set of executive actions offers different types of immigration relief to different subgroups of the unauthorized population. The beneficiary groups reflect the general priority the U.S. immigration system gives to preserving the unity of the immediate families of U.S. citizens and LPRs. None of the executive actions directly grant beneficiaries a lawful immigration status – only congressional action can confer immigration status.

The expansion of the provisional unlawful presence waiver program to specified relatives of U.S. citizens and LPRs—spouses and minor children of LPRs and adult children of U.S. citizens and LPRs—with approved immigrant visa petitions could help facilitate these individuals' acquisition of LPR status. Beneficiaries of approved immigrant petitions who are unable to adjust status in the United States would still need to return to their home countries in order to pursue LPR status. Before leaving the United States to apply for a visa abroad, however, an eligible individual could apply for and receive a provisional unlawful presence waiver. During the overseas visa process, if a consular officer determines that the individual is subject to a 3- or 10-year bar on admission—and that no other grounds of inadmissibility apply—the individual could use the waiver to obtain a visa and gain admission to the United States as an LPR.

The executive action on advance parole also addresses the 3- and 10-year bars, but in a different way. It effectively would make the 3- and 10-year bars inapplicable in cases in which an individual leaves the United States after being granted advance parole and then seeks to return.

The expansion of the military parole-in-place program would enable eligible spouses, children, and parents of U.S. citizens and LPRs who seek to enlist in the U.S. Armed Forces to be granted parole. Although parole is not considered an immigration status, an individual with parole can adjust to LPR status in the United States provided that he or she meets the applicable requirements (see "Provisional Unlawful Presence Waivers").

The expansion of eligibility for DACA and the establishment of a new deferred action process for the unauthorized parents of U.S. citizens and LPRs who meet specified requirements could enable individuals in the newly covered groups to remain in the United States and, if granted employment authorization, to work legally. During the period of deferred action, these individuals would have protection from removal. They would be in a period of stay authorized by DHS and would be considered to be lawfully present for admissibility purposes. As such, during the period of deferred action, they would not accrue unlawful presence for admissibility purposes (which is relevant for application of the 3- and 10-year bars). Individuals granted deferred action would not be provided with a pathway to a lawful immigration status, however, and DHS has the discretion to terminate the grant of deferred action at any time.

High-Skilled Workers

A key principle underlying U.S. immigration policy is facilitating the permanent and temporary entry of foreign nationals with needed skills.

Admitting professional, managerial, and skilled foreign workers raises a series of policy tensions as the United States attempts to compete internationally for the most talented workers without negatively impacting wages and working conditions of native workers and students entering the U.S. labor market.[76]

Permanent Employment-Based Immigration[77]

Immigrant admissions and adjustments for LPR status are subject to a complex set of numerical limits and preference categories that give priority for admission on the basis of family relationships, needed skills, and geographic diversity. The current employment-based LPR visa system consists of five numerically limited preference categories:

- *first preference*: priority workers who are persons of extraordinary ability in the arts, the sciences, education, business, or athletics; outstanding professors and researchers; and certain multinational executives and managers;
- *second preference*: members of the professions holding advanced degrees or persons of exceptional ability;
- *third preference*: skilled workers with at least two years training, professionals with baccalaureate degrees, and unskilled workers in occupations in which U.S. workers are in short supply;
- *fourth preference*: special immigrants who largely consist of religious workers, certain former employees of the U.S. government, and undocumented juveniles who become wards of the court; and
- *fifth preference*: investors who invest at least $1 million (or less money in rural areas or areas of high unemployment) to create at least 10 new jobs.

Employers who seek to hire prospective immigrant workers petition USCIS. Employers who seek to hire prospective employment-based immigrants through the second and third preference categories also must petition the U.S. Department of Labor (DOL) on behalf of the alien (see "Labor Certification" below).[78]

High-Skilled Temporary Worker Visas[79]

Temporary visas for professional, managerial, and skilled foreign workers have become an important gateway for high-skilled permanent immigration to the United States.[80] The Administration contends that employers use temporary worker visas to retain workers as they wait for LPR visa numbers to become available. If workers' nonimmigrant visas expire before their permanent visas become available, such workers must leave the country.[81]

Over the past two decades, the number of visas issued for temporary employment-based workers has more than doubled, from just over 400,000 in FY1994 to over 1 million in FY2013.[82] Notably, policy makers and advocates have focused on two visa categories in particular: H-1B visas for professional specialty workers and L visas for intracompany transferees. These two nonimmigrant visas epitomize the tensions between the global competition for talent and possible adverse effects on U.S. workers.

Changes to Current Policy

On November 20, 2014, the DHS Secretary released a policy memorandum stating that USCIS will be producing new regulations and policies designed to "grow our economy and create jobs" by attracting and retaining highly skilled immigrants.[83] The policy changes will affect employment-based LPR visas; optional practical training (OPT) for foreign students; the L visa category for intracompany transfers; and select foreign nationals who are inventors, researchers, and founders of start-up enterprises.[84] In addition, the Secretary announced that he will be publishing a final rule to incentivize employers of current temporary workers to sponsor them for LPR status. Concurrently, DOL announced a review of the policies and regulations related to labor certification.[85]

Preventing Visa Retrogression[86]

As discussed above, a complex set of numerical limits and preference categories dictate how many and which persons may become LPRs in a given year. DOS is responsible for allocating the visas based on family- and employment-based preference categories and uniform per-country limits. DOS must calculate when a visa number is available for a specific foreign national with an approved immigrant petition, allowing that foreign national to adjust to LPR status if they are in the United States or receive their LPR visa if they are outside the country. Several years ago, "accounting problems" between USCIS's processing of LPR adjustments of status in the United States and Consular Affairs' processing of LPR visas abroad became apparent.[87] This difference unexpectedly lengthened the wait for a visa for some foreign nationals with approved LPR applications (i.e., visa retrogression).[88]

In the High-Skilled Memorandum, the Secretary states that USCIS should continue to work with DOS to make sure that all immigrant visas are allocated when there is demand for such visas, and improve the system for determining when visas become available. DOS reportedly has agreed to modify the visa bulletin to clarify when a person's visa number will become available.

Labor Certification

The INA bars the admission of prospective immigrants who seek to enter the United States to perform skilled or unskilled labor, unless the Secretary of Labor certifies to the Secretaries of State and Homeland Security that such foreign workers will not displace or adversely affect the working conditions of U.S. workers.[89] All labor certification applications (LCAs) for aliens seeking LPR status are processed through DOL's Program Electronic Review Management (PERM) labor certification system.[90] In FY2014, employers reportedly submitted over 70,000 PERM applications requesting foreign workers, and the majority of the job openings were for professional occupations in Information Technology and Science.[91] Under the President's executive action, DOL will review the PERM program and relevant regulations, with the goal of making the program more responsive to changes in the national work force.[92]

Changing Jobs

Currently, employees with pending employment-based LPR visa applications may change jobs without jeopardizing their application only if the new job or position is in a "same or similar" occupational classification. Reportedly, workers often will not accept promotions or change employers due to fear of invalidating their applications.[93] Under the High-Skilled Memorandum, USCIS was directed to consider amending regulations to ensure that long-standing visa petitions are not invalidated in cases where the employee seeks to change jobs or employers. Specifically, the DHS Secretary directed USCIS to issue a policy memorandum that provides guidance on the definition of "same or similar" occupational classification.

National Interest Waiver

Generally, foreign nationals attempting to immigrate under the second and third employment- based preference categories must be sponsored by an employer, who must certify that the foreign national is not displacing U.S. workers. Under the INA, certain foreign nationals with advanced degrees or exceptional ability may apply for LPR status without an employer sponsor if it is in the national interest.[94] This is known as the "national interest waiver."[95] According to the Administration, the waiver is underutilized and limited guidance exists on its use. In the High Skilled Memorandum, the DHS Secretary directs USCIS to issue guidance or regulations clarifying the circumstances under which the national interest waiver can be used.

Start up Visas

Some have criticized the fifth-preference employment-based (EB-5) visa category for not allowing its applicants, who generate business ideas and obtain investor backing to launch them, to petition for LPR status.[96] In the 113th Congress, House-passed H.R. 2131 and Senate-passed S.744 would have, under certain circumstances, allowed foreign nationals who received investment money from qualified investors to apply for LPR status.

The DHS Secretary, through the High-Skilled Memorandum, directs USCIS to create a program using the "significant public benefit" parole authority[97] to allow certain high-skilled foreign nationals to enter or remain in the United States. The program would grant parole on a case-by- case basis to investors, researchers, and founders of start-up enterprises who may not qualify for the public interest waiver or EB-5 status, but who have secured "substantial" financing from U.S. investors or who "otherwise hold the promise of innovation and job creation through the development of new technologies or the pursuit of 'cutting edge' research."

According to the memorandum, the grant of parole would temporarily allow these foreign nationals to pursue research, new ideas, and businesses in the United States rather than abroad, and give them time to secure temporary or permanent immigration statuses. Regulations to implement this program must include income and resource requirements. In addition, those who receive parole under this program will, reportedly, be ineligible for federal public benefits[98] and premium tax credits under the Affordable Care Act.[99]

Optional Practical Training (OPT)

During or after completing their undergraduate or graduate studies, foreign students on F-1 visas are permitted to participate in employment known as Optional Practical Training (OPT).[100] OPT is temporary employment that is directly related to an F-1 student's major area of study.

Generally, an F-1 foreign student may work up to 12 months in OPT status. In 2008, DHS expanded the OPT work period to 29 months for F-1 students in STEM fields.[101]

The High-Skilled Memorandum directs USCIS and ICE to develop regulations to expand the number of degree programs eligible for OPT, and to extend the time period and use of OPT for STEM students and graduates. The new policy will also require the OPT program to have stronger ties to degree-granting institutions to ensure that a student's OPT furthers his or her course of study in the United States. In addition, the new policy is to be consistent with U.S. worker protections.

L Visas[102]

Current law permits intracompany transferees to enter the United States on a nonimmigrant L visa that is designed for executives, managers, or employees with specialized knowledge of a firm's products. The L visa permits multinational firms to transfer top-level personnel to their locations in the United States for up to seven years.[103] The INA does not require firms wishing to bring L intracompany transfers into the United States to demonstrate that U.S. workers will not be adversely affected in order to obtain L visas.

The L visa category is considered essential to retaining and expanding international businesses in the United States. Some, however, have raised concerns that intracompany transferees on the L visa may displace U.S. workers who had been employed in those positions for these firms in the United States. Others contend that the L visa has become a substitute for the H-1B visa, noting that L visa employees are often comparable in skills and occupations to H-1B workers yet lack the latter's labor market protections. These concerns have often been raised with certain outsourcing and information technology firms that employ L visa workers as subcontractors within the United States. A related concern is that the unchecked use of L visas will foster the transfer of STEM and other high-skilled professional jobs overseas.[104] After investigating the L visa, the DHS Inspector General offered this assessment: "That so many foreign workers seem to qualify as possessing specialized knowledge appears to have led to the displacement of American workers, and to what is sometimes called the 'body shop' problem."[105]

In the High-Skilled Memorandum, the DHS Secretary directs USCIS to issue a policy clarifying the meaning of "specialized knowledge" for L visa qualification. Reportedly, the goal of the new policy guidance is to yield more consistent adjudication outcomes.[106]

Discussion

The Administration did not provide details about the proposed policy changes related to high- skilled workers, but rather directed agencies to develop policies and regulations in these areas. Until such details are clarified, the potential impact of the changes remains unclear.

INTEGRATION AND NATURALIZATION

Immigrant Integration

Immigrant integration refers to the process by which immigrants become socially, economically, culturally, and politically integrated into American society.[107] The United States admits for permanent residence, and processes for citizenship, the largest proportion and absolute number of foreign nationals of any other major immigrant-receiving nation. As the foreign-born population in the United States increases—41.3 million persons or 13.1% of the total U.S. population in 2013—federally funded immigrant integration programs take on greater prominence.

Unlike other major immigrant-receiving nations, the United States has no national policy or dedicated executive branch office focused on coordinating immigrant integration efforts across federal agencies.[108] Federal immigrant integration programs take direct and indirect forms. Direct forms include the Department of Education's English Language Acquisition Grants and Migrant Education Programs, and the DHS Office of Citizenship's Immigrant Integration and Citizenship Program. Indirect forms are more numerous and often provide assistance to mostly low-income individuals.[109] States and localities also contend with immigrant integration, particularly in new immigrant destination states. Increasing numbers of states and localities grapple with issues of communication and English language learning as well as law enforcement, education, workforce development, adult literacy, and health access, among others.

Immigration advocates contend that the size and growth of the foreign-born population and the need for greater efficiency and integration among federal and state agencies warrants an executive branch office for immigrant integration.[110] A number of task forces have been convened to address this issue.[111] Immigration advocates contend, however, that such proposals must go farther by establishing a federal office to coordinate and facilitate immigrant integration nationally in a more comprehensive manner.[112] The Senate's comprehensive immigration reform bill, S. 744, included such broader provisions.[113]

The President's executive action establishes an interagency "White House Task Force on New Americans" with two primary objectives: (1) identify, promote, and expand immigrant integration best practices within states and localities; and (2) help determine steps that federal agencies can take to improve their own immigrant integration efforts.[114] Other functions outlined within the action include: providing technical assistance and training; collecting and disseminating related data and information; soliciting recommendations from nonprofit organizations, government officials and other stakeholders; and monitoring equitable access to integration programs. The task force is expected to provide the President with recommendations to further the civic, economic, and linguistic integration of new Americans within four months and an implementation status report within a year.

Encouraging Naturalization

Naturalization, the process that grants U.S. citizenship to LPRs, is often viewed as a milestone for immigrants and a measure of their socioeconomic integration and assimilation to the United States. Practically, naturalized immigrants gain important benefits, including the right to vote, security from deportation in most cases, access to certain public-sector jobs, and the ability to travel with a U.S. passport.[115] U.S. citizens are also advantaged over LPRs for sponsoring relatives to immigrate to the United States.

Despite the clear benefits of U.S. citizenship status over LPR status, millions of LPRs who are eligible to naturalize do not do so. Part of the reason for this may stem from INA requirements for naturalization that include five years of continuous residence in the United States, possession of "good moral character" and English language competency, and the passing of a U.S. government and history examination as part of a naturalization interview.[116]

Naturalization applicants must also pay a fee, which some observers argue hinders LPRs from acquiring citizenship.[117] USCIS currently charges $680 to process naturalization petitions. The fee amount raises several issues for Congress, including whether it is sufficiently onerous that it discourages naturalization, and whether it accurately reflects USCIS's cost to process naturalization applications. Empirical studies suggest that the volume of naturalization petitions filed may be inversely related to the naturalization fee amount,[118] although other factors also explain application volume increases apart from fee increases.[119] Immigration advocates have proposed providing more payment options for naturalization fees and making information about fee waivers more widely known.[120]

The President's executive action directs USCIS to accept credit cards as a payment option for the naturalization fee, in addition to money orders or checks (which are currently the only payment options).[121] The action also directs USCIS to consider the feasibility of a partial fee waiver to the naturalization fee. While USCIS offers waivers for some of its immigration services fees, waivers for the $680 naturalization fee are currently available only to those whose income is less than or equal to 150% of the federal poverty level. Those with incomes above this level do not qualify for any waiver and must pay the full $680 fee.

Discussion

How the President's creation of the White House Task force on New Americans marks a significant departure from previous federal efforts that explicitly focused on immigrant integration is unclear. Because it originates from an executive action, it lacks funding from Congress. While some advances may result from greater federal coordination, the actual integration of immigrants into American society—economically, politically, socially, and culturally—involves considerable time and effort across many policy areas. Some immigration observers, citing experiences of earlier generations of immigrants, argue that taxpayers should not be funding government initiatives to foster integration. Others view some integration programs, such as English language instruction, as valuable investments that yield positive long-term returns.

Promoting naturalization generally has wide support, and expanding payment options for the naturalization fee may provide greater convenience for potential naturalization petitioners. Empirical evidence also suggests that the propensity to naturalize is price sensitive, suggesting that naturalization fee waiver options may boost naturalization rates among those who otherwise would not apply. Any such waiver options, however, will require USCIS to make up the corresponding shortfall in fee revenue through other means, including, possibly, reducing services, increasing processing times, and increasing other processing fees.

OTHER EXECUTIVE ACTION INITIATIVES

Modernizing the U.S. Immigrant Visa System

Many agree that the U.S. immigration system contains dysfunctions for those who petition for immigration services and benefits: it is complicated to understand, redundant, time-consuming, and costly and burdensome to applicants and businesses. Some argue that the system, which requires technological infrastructure beyond what its fee structure can support,[122] has reached a level that thwarts effective administration.[123]

Bureaucratic and legal complexity can be expected of an administrative, technical, and legal system that handles the range of immigrant circumstances found in the United States, as well as the corresponding range of goals and objectives of agencies charged with implementing and enforcing U.S. immigration law. Yet, unlike regularly proposed and attempted overhauls of the similarly complex tax system, no major attempts have been made to overhaul the U.S. immigration system to allow it to work more efficiently and expediently.[124]

USCIS, the DHS agency responsible for processing and adjudicating immigration petitions, has for several years undertaken a "modernization" program intended to convert itself from an entirely paper-based agency to a mostly digital platform. A recent review by DHS's Office of the Inspector General suggested that the program's goals have not yet been met.[125]

On November 21, the White House, as part of the President's executive action, directed the Secretaries of State and Homeland Security in consultation with other federal agencies and stakeholders to recommend ways to (1) improve and streamline the legal immigration system, emphasizing reforms that reduce government costs, improve services for applicants, reduce employer burdens, and reduce waste and fraud; (2) ensure that all the visa numbers are used; and (3) modernize the visa processing technology to reduce redundancy, improve applicants' experiences and increase public oversight. The secretaries are also to establish metrics that can quantify improvement in these three areas.[126]

Such reforms, long desired, will become more critical for USCIS as it implements the President's executive action. Soliciting recommendations for improving the functioning of the immigration system may help alleviate some challenges faced by end users. As with other components of the President's initiative, it remains to be seen how much can be accomplished through administrative refinements and the deployment of existing resources without the benefit of additional funding.

More Consistent Enforcement of Federal Labor, Employment, and Immigration Laws

In 2012, an estimated 8.1 million unauthorized aliens, representing just over 5% of the U.S. workforce, were working or looking for work in the United States.[127] Lacking proper work authorization, they are vulnerable to exploitation in a variety of ways and less likely to have sufficient resources to enforce their rights effectively.[128]

Three sources of labor protections exist for foreign workers in the United States: (1) conditions imposed on employers hiring foreign workers through the labor certification-attestation portion of the petition to admit foreign workers; (2) federal labor laws regarding employer adherence to requirements for wages and working conditions; and (3) private causes of action that foreign workers may have under state and local laws.[129] DOL, which is responsible for enforcing minimum wage, overtime pay, and related requirements, focuses a significant percentage of its enforcement resources on low-wage industries that employ large numbers of immigrant—and presumably large numbers of unauthorized—workers. [130] Among other tasks, ICE is responsible for investigating immigration law violations related to knowingly hiring unauthorized aliens.[131]

In April 2009, DHS issued new guidance on immigration-related worksite enforcement that "reflects a renewed Department-wide focus targeting criminal aliens and employers who cultivate illegal workplaces by breaking the country's laws and knowingly hiring illegal workers."[132] In December 2011, DHS and DOL signed a revised memorandum of understanding to coordinate worksite enforcement actions and make them consistent with each agency's mission.[133] Questions have arisen as to how rigorous and effective DHS's worksite enforcement efforts are and have been in past years.[134]

On November 21, 2014, as part of the President's executive action, DOL announced the creation of an inter-agency working group to "promote effective and consistent enforcement of federal labor, employment, and immigration laws, with the goal of protecting all workers regardless of legal status." [135] The working group will include representatives from federal agencies responsible for immigration enforcement and worker protections, including the Departments of Labor, Homeland Security, and Justice, and the

Equal Employment Opportunity Commission and National Labor Relations Board.

The working group is broadly tasked with ensuring that (1) current immigration and employment policies do not dissuade workers from cooperating with law enforcement authorities in cases of employment violations; (2) federal enforcement authorities are not used by those who wish to undermine worker protections by enmeshing immigration authorities in labor disputes; and (3) federal labor, employment, and immigration laws are consistently applied.

As with most of the other elements of the President's executive action, this initiative is being implemented without a congressional appropriation or stated source of funding. Hence, it remains to be seen the extent to which the creation of an inter-agency task force and greater coordination and planning among and within agencies can improve wages and worksite conditions for workers vulnerable to exploitation because of their immigration status (or lack thereof).

Expanding Support for Crime Victims

U nonimmigrant status is reserved for victims of certain statutorily specified crimes that occurred within the United States.[136] To qualify for U status, a foreign national must receive certification from a law enforcement agency that he or she is being or is likely to be helpful in the investigation and prosecution of the criminal activity.

T nonimmigrant status is reserved for foreign nationals in the United States who are victims of severe forms of trafficking. To receive it, foreign nationals, with some exceptions, must comply with reasonable requests for assistance from law enforcement. Law enforcement certification is optional for T status, unlike for U status, but it serves as important evidence for applicants.[137]

As part of the President's executive actions, the Department of Labor (DOL) has announced that in early 2015 it will begin exercising its authority to provide law enforcement certification to trafficking victims applying for T status.[138] In addition, DOL will simultaneously expand the types of crimes for which it certifies to include victims of extortion, forced labor, and foreign labor contracting fraud.[139]

The DOL Wage and Hour Division enforces federal labor laws, including the Fair Labor Standards Act and the Migrant and Seasonal Agricultural

Workers Protection Act, and assists with human trafficking investigations involving violations of these laws. As a result, DOL may encounter trafficking victims. Some advocates note that DOL's enforcement of wage and hour laws could help reveal trafficking and crime victims, as those who engage in labor trafficking or other criminal activity in the workplace are also likely to violate wage and hour laws.[140]

CONCLUSION

The President's Immigration Accountability Executive Action announced on November 20, 2014, includes provisions meant to alleviate uncertainty for potentially millions of unauthorized aliens through deferred action and the use of provisional waivers and parole. It is also intended to revise enforcement priorities and improve and coordinate strategic initiatives across a range of immigration policy areas, including border security, high skilled immigration, and naturalization. Whether this executive action can accomplish these objectives and prompt Congress to pass more permanent legislative solutions is unclear.

Accomplishing such goals in the face of a potentially resistant Congress may prove challenging. USCIS, the agency tasked with carrying out sizable portions of the executive action, will be relying upon an indeterminate amount of additional fee revenue from deferred action petitions to implement some of these objectives, while other agencies, lacking congressional appropriations, will be attempting to implement changes to current policies and procedures mostly through increased coordination and more innovative marshaling of existing resources.

End Notes

[1] Migration Policy Institute, *MPI: As Many as 3.7 Million Unauthorized Immigrants Could Get Relief from Deportation under Anticipated New Deferred Action Program - With Existing DACA Program Included, Anticipated Actions Could Benefit More than 5.2 Million in Total — Nearly Half of U.S. Unauthorized Population*, Press Release, November 30, 2014. The press release is based upon analytic work presented in Randy Capps, Marc R. Rosenblum, and James D. Bachmeier, *Executive Action for Unauthorized Immigrants: Estimates of the Populations that Could Receive Relief*, Migration Policy Institute, Issue Brief No. 10, Washington, DC, September 2014.

[2] For more information on this debate, see CRS Report R43782, *Executive Discretion as to Immigration: Legal Overview*, by Kate M. Manuel and Michael John Garcia.

[3] For example, see a discussion of broad immigration debates surrounding family-based immigration in CRS Report R43145, *U.S. Family-Based Immigration Policy*, by William A. Kandel.

[4] CRS Report R41207, *Unauthorized Aliens in the United States: Policy Discussion*, by Andorra Bruno.

[5] See archived CRS Report R42530, *Immigration of Foreign Nationals with Science, Technology, Engineering, and Mathematics (STEM) Degrees* , by Ruth Ellen Wasem.

[6] CRS Report R42866, *Permanent Legal Immigration to the United States: Policy Overview*, by William A. Kandel.

[7] CRS Report R42969, *Border Security: Understanding Threats at U.S. Borders*, by Jerome P. Bjelopera and Kristin Finklea; CRS Report R43356, *Border Security: Immigration Inspections at Ports of Entry*, by Lisa Seghetti; CRS Report R42138, *Border Security: Immigration Enforcement Between Ports of Entry*, by Lisa Seghetti; CRS Report R42057, *Interior Immigration Enforcement: Programs Targeting Criminal Aliens*, by Marc R. Rosenblum and William A. Kandel.

[8] In the 113th Congress, House committees reported or ordered to be reported the following immigration bills: Border Security Results Act of 2013 (H.R. 1417); Strengthen and Fortify Enforcement (SAFE) Act (H.R. 2278); Legal Workforce Act (H.R. 1772); Agricultural Guestworker (AG) Act (H.R. 1773); and Supplying Knowledge-based Immigrants and Lifting Levels of STEM Visas (SKILLS Visa) Act (H.R. 2131).

[9] For more information, see CRS Report R42138, *Border Security: Immigration Enforcement Between Ports of Entry*, by Lisa Seghetti.

[10] These include a network of ground sensors, agent-centric mobile surveillance equipment, integrated fixed towers, agent-portable tripod-mounted surveillance systems, vehicle-mounted mobile surveillance systems, truck-mounted mobile vehicle surveillance systems, tower-mounted remote video surveillance systems, and air-based surveillance systems, all of which are linked, to varying degrees, to centralized control rooms where personnel monitor the border, alert field agents to potential incursions, and coordinate the response. In recent years, the Border Patrol's focus with respect to surveillance technology has shifted from fixed towers and other static resources to more mobile and dynamic systems. From CRS discussions with U.S. Border Patrol, December 17, 2012 and August 26, 2014; also see U.S. Border Patrol, *2012-2016 Border Patrol Strategic Plan*, Washington, DC: 2012.

[11] CBP houses much of this capacity in its "Office of Air and Marine. . .[which] is the world's largest aviation and maritime law enforcement organization, a critical component of CBP's layered enforcement strategy for border security. [The Office of Air and Marine has] 1,200 federal agents, more than 250 aircraft and over 280 marine vessels operating from 83 locations in the United States and Puerto Rico. See http://www.cbp.gov/border-security/air-sea.

[12] This includes items such as fencing and lighting along the border. In addition to fencing and other infrastructure in the immediate border region, DHS deploys a variety of checkpoints and forward operating bases to enhance border security. Checkpoints, including permanent and "tactical" (or roving) checkpoints, are located at some distance from the linear border, usually within 100 miles of the border.

[13] See for example, Jeh Charles Johnson, Secretary, Department of Homeland Security, "Border Security in the 21st Century," public remarks delivered at the Center for Strategic and International Studies, Washington, D.C., October 9, 2014. Hereafter Johnson, "Border Security in the 21st Century." White House, "Fixing the Immigration System for America's 21st Century Economy."

[14] See, for example, Tom Howell, Jr, "Senate Republicans: Immigration Reform Must Deal First with Border Security," *Washington Times,* November 19, 2014; Alan Gomez, "Border Security Quandary Could Kill Immigration Bill," *USA Today*, April 2, 2013.

[15] Johnson, "Border Security in the 21st Century."

[16] CBP, *2012-2016 Border Patrol Strategic Plan*, Washington, DC: 2012, p. 7.

[17] Ibid.

[18] Office of Air and Marine and the Office of Field Operations (CBP officers at POEs).

[19] Joint written testimony of Custom and Border Protection's U.S. Border Patrol Chief Michael Fisher, (then) Office of Air and Marine Assistant Commissioner Michael Kostelnik, Office of Technology Innovation & Acquisition Assistant Commissioner Mark Borkowski, and (then) Office of Field Operations Acting Assistant Commissioner Kevin McAleenan for a House Committee on Appropriations, Subcommittee on Homeland Security hearing on The President's Fiscal Year 2013 budget request for CBP, February 29, 2012.

[20] U.S. Department of Homeland Security, Memorandum to R. Gil Kerlikowske, Commissioner, U.S. Customs and Border Protection, Admiral Paul F. Zukunft, Commandant, U.S. Coast Guard, Thomas S. Winkowski, Acting Director, U.S. Immigration and Customs Enforcement, Leon Rodriquez, Director, U.S. Citizenship and Immigration Services, W. Craig Fugate, Administrator, Federal Emergency Management Agency, and Alan D. Bersin, Acting Assistant Secretary for Policy, from Jeh Charles Johnson, Secretary of Homeland Security, *Southern Border and Approaches Campaign*, November 20, 2014.

[21] Ibid.

[22] According to the November 20, 2014 memo, the Task Forces "should adopt a supported-supporting component model. Among the Components of this Department [DHS], CBP will be the supported component in Joint Task Force West, the USCG will be the supported component in Joint Task Force East, and ICE will be the supported component in Joint Task Force Investigations."

[23] In the civil immigration enforcement context, the term "prosecutorial discretion" applies to a broad range of discretionary enforcement decisions including issuing or canceling notices to appear (NTAs) which start the removal process, allowing other forms of removal (e.g., voluntary departure), rather than instituting a standard removal proceeding in immigration court, granting deferred action and deciding whom to arrest for a violation of civil immigration law. Prosecutorial discretion may be exercised at any stage of an enforcement proceeding, but policy states that it should generally be exercised as early in the case as possible to preserve government resources.

[24] DHS personnel who are authorized to initiate removal procedures include U.S. Customs and Border Protection (CBP) officers and U.S. Border Patrol agents (within CBP), asylum and examination officers in U.S. Citizenship and Immigration Services (USCIS), and detention officers and other agents in U.S. Immigration and Customs Enforcement (ICE); see 8 C.F.R. §239.1(a).

[25] U.S. Department of Homeland Security, Memorandum to Thomas S. Winkowski, Acting Director, U.S. Immigration and Customs Enforcement, R. Gil Kerlikowske, Commissioner, U.S. Customs and Border Protection, Leon Rodriquez, Director, U.S. Citizenship and Immigration Services, and Alan D. Bersin, Acting Assistant Secretary for Policy, from Jeh Charles Johnson, Secretary of Homeland Security, *Policies for the Apprehension, Detention, and Removal of Undocumented Immigrants*, November 20, 2014; and U.S. Department of Homeland Security, Memorandum to Thomas S. Winkowski, Acting Director, U.S. Immigration and Customs Enforcement, Megan Mack, Officer, Officer of Civil Rights and Civil Liberties, and Philip A. McNamara, Assistant Secretary, Intergovernmental Affairs, from Jeh Charles Johnson, Secretary of Homeland Security, *Secure Communities*, November 20, 2014.

[26] U.S. Department of Homeland Security, Memorandum to Thomas S. Winkowski, Acting Director, U.S. Immigration and Customs Enforcement, and Catherine Emerson, Chief Human Capital Officer, Department of Homeland Security, from Jeh Charles Johnson, Secretary of Homeland Security, *Personnel Reform for Immigration and Customs Enforcement Officers*, November 20, 2014.

[27] U.S. Department of Homeland Security, Memorandum to Thomas S. Winkowski, Acting Director, U.S. Immigration and Customs Enforcement, R. Gil Kerlikowske, Commissioner, U.S. Customs and Border Protection, Leon Rodriquez, Director, U.S. Citizenship and

Immigration Services, and Alan D. Bersin, Acting Assistant Secretary for Policy, from Jeh Charles Johnson, Secretary of Homeland Security, *Policies for the Apprehension, Detention, and Removal of Undocumented Immigrants*, November 20, 2014, p. 2.

[28] Criminal street gang is defined in 18 U.S.C. §521(a).

[29] Felonies include any offense classified as a felony in the convicting jurisdiction, and any aggravated felony as defined in INA §101(a)(43).

[30] This excludes traffic offenses.

[31] Significant misdemeanor is defined as an offense of domestic violence, sexual abuse or exploitation; burglary; unlawful possession or use of a firearm; drug distribution or trafficking; or driving under the influence; or one for which the individual was sentenced to time in custody for 90 days or more.

[32] The policy leaves room for discretion among DHS personnel, even with *Priority 1* aliens. The policy states that an alien should be prioritized for removal unless he or she may be eligible for relief from removal or factors exist that, in the judgment of DHS personnel, indicate the person should not be an enforcement priority. Notably, *Priority 1* requires "compelling and exceptional factors that clearly indicate the alien is not a threat to national security, border security, or public safety and should not therefore be an enforcement priority," while *Priority 3* requires "the alien is not a threat to the integrity of the immigration system or there are factors suggesting the alien should not be an enforcement priority."

[33] John Morton, *Memorandum on Civil Immigration Enforcement: Priorities for the Apprehension, Detention, and Removal of Aliens*, U.S. Immigration and Customs Enforcement, Washington, DC, March 2, 2011; John Morton, *Exercising Prosecutorial Discretion Consistent with the Civil Immigration Enforcement Priorities of the Agency for the Apprehension, Detention, and Removal of Aliens*, U.S. Department of Homeland Security Immigration and Customs Enforcement, Washington, DC, June 17, 2011; and John Morton, *Prosecutorial Discretion: Certain Victims, Witnesses, and Plaintiffs*, U.S. Department of Homeland Security Immigration and Customs Enforcement, Washington, DC, June 17, 2011.

[34] Although the immigration agencies have issued guidance regarding enforcement priorities since at least 1975, analysis of the evolution of enforcement priorities is beyond the scope of this report.

[35] Aliens who have been issued final orders of removal but who have not departed from the United States are known as absconders or fugitive aliens. Since FY2002, there has been a concerted effort to remove absconders. In 2003, Congress mandated that the names of absconders be added to DOJ's National Crime Information System. See archived CRS Report RL33351, *Immigration Enforcement Within the United States*, coordinated by Alison Siskin, and CRS Report R42057, *Interior Immigration Enforcement: Programs Targeting Criminal Aliens*, by Marc R. Rosenblum and William A. Kandel.

[36] John Morton, *Memorandum on Civil Immigration Enforcement: Priorities for the Apprehension, Detention, and Removal of Aliens*, U.S. Immigration and Customs Enforcement, Washington, DC, March 2, 2011.

[37] Under statute, those subject to mandatory detention include criminal aliens, national security risks, certain arriving aliens, and select persons with final orders of removal. For more on mandatory detention, see CRS Report RL32369, *Immigration-Related Detention*, by Alison Siskin, and CRS Report WSLG524, *How "Mandatory" Is the Mandatory Detention of Certain Aliens in Removal Proceedings,* by Michael John Garcia.

[38] For example, see Mark Hugo Lopez, Ana Gonzalez-Barrera, and Seth Motel, *As Deportations Rise to Record Levels, Most Latinos Oppose Obama's Policy*, Pew Research Hispanic Trends Project, Washington, DC, December 28, 2011, Appendix A.

[39] For example, see Jessica Vaughan, *Deportation Numbers Unwrapped: Raw Statistics Reveal the Real Story of ICE Enforcement in Decline*, Center for Immigration Studies, Washington, DC, October 2013; and Brian Bennett, "High Deportation Figures are Misleading," *LA Times*, April 1, 2014, p. 1.

[40] Chuck Wexler et al., *Taskforce on Secure Communities Findings and Recommendations*, Homeland Security Advisory Council, Washington, DC, September 2011, p. 11; and ICE, *Congressional Budget Justification FY2014*, p. 57.

[41] DOJ's Integrated Automated Fingerprint Identification System (IAFIS) conducts criminal and terrorist background checks in response to requests from federal, state, and local law enforcement agencies by checking fingerprints against the IAFIS database of fingerprints, criminal histories, photographs, and biographic information. See Federal Bureau of Investigation, "Integrated Automated Fingerprint Identification System," http://www.fbi.gov/about-us/cjis/ fingerprints_biometrics/iafis/iafis.

[42] The IDENT database is DHS's primary department-wide biometric database, and includes photographs, fingerprints, biographic name, personal identifier data, citizenship and nationality, and derogatory information, if applicable. See DHS, *Privacy Impact Assessment for the Automated Biometric Identification System (IDENT),* Dec. 7, 2012.

[43] Chuck Wexler et al., *Taskforce on Secure Communities Findings and Recommendations*, Homeland Security Advisory Council, Washington, DC, September 2011, p. 10.

[44] The Criminal Alien Program (CAP) is an umbrella program that includes several different systems for identifying, detaining, and initiating removal proceedings against criminal aliens incarcerated within federal, state, and local prisons and jails, as well as at-large criminal aliens that have been released into communities after serving their sentences. Immigration and Customs Enforcement, Enforcement and Removal Operations, *Crimnal Alien Program*, Fact Sheet, Washington, DC, http://www.ice.gov/ criminal-alien-program. See also CRS Report R42057, *Interior Immigration Enforcement: Programs Targeting Criminal Aliens*, by Marc R. Rosenblum and William A. Kandel.

[45] U.S. Department of Homeland Security, Memorandum to Thomas S. Winkowski, Acting Director, U.S. Immigration and Customs Enforcement, Megan Mack, Officer, Office of Civil Rights and Civil Liberties, and Philip A. McNamara, Assistant Secretary for Intergovernmental Affairs, from Jeh Charles Johnson, Secretary of Homeland Security, *Secure Communities*, November 20, 2014.

[46] ICE and its predecessor, the Immigration and Naturalization Service (INS), have used detainers as one means of obtaining custody of aliens for removal proceedings since at least 1950. CRS Report R42690, *Immigration Detainers: Legal Issues*, by Kate M. Manuel.

[47] See CRS Report R42690, *Immigration Detainers: Legal Issues*, by Kate M. Manuel.

[48] Chuck Wexler et al., *Taskforce on Secure Communities Findings and Recommendations*, Homeland Security Advisory Council, Washington, DC, September 2011, p. 26.

[49] U.S. Department of Homeland Security, Memorandum to Thomas S. Winkowski, Acting Director, U.S. Immigration and Customs Enforcement, and Catherine Emerson, Chief Human Capital Officer, Department of Homeland Security, from Jeh Charles Johnson, Secretary of Homeland Security, *Personnel Reform for Immigration and Customs Enforcement Officers*, November 20, 2014, p. 2.

[50] Ibid, p. 1.

[51] Dan Cadman, *Analysis of Obama's Executive Amnesty Scheme: ICE Personnel Reform*, Center for Immigration Studies, Washington, DC, December 2, 2014.

[52] Aliens who have been issued final orders of removal but who have not departed from the United States are known as absconders or fugitive aliens. In 2003, Congress mandated that the names of absconders be added to DOJ's National Crime Information System. See archived CRS Report RL33351, *Immigration Enforcement Within the United States*, coordinated by Alison Siskin, and CRS Report R42057, *Interior Immigration Enforcement: Programs Targeting Criminal Aliens*, by Marc R. Rosenblum and William A. Kandel.

[53] ICE, *Congressional Budget Justification FY2015*, pp. 52-53.

[54] *Alien* is a term in U.S. immigration law that is synonymous with *foreign national* and *noncitizen*.

[55] See CRS Report RL33863, *Unauthorized Alien Students: Issues and "DREAM Act" Legislation*, by Andorra Bruno.

[56] Border Security, Economic Opportunity, and Immigration Modernization Act (S. 744). See CRS Report R43097, *Comprehensive Immigration Reform in the 113th Congress: Major Provisions in Senate-Passed S. 744*, by Ruth Ellen Wasem. CRS Report R43782, *Executive Discretion as to Immigration: Legal Overview*, by Kate M. Manuel and Michael John Garcia.

[57] For a discussion of related legal issues, see CRS Report R43798, *The Obama Administration's November 2014 Immigration Initiatives: Questions and Answers*, by Kate M. Manuel; and CRS Report R43782, *Executive Discretion as to Immigration: Legal Overview*, by Kate M. Manuel and Michael John Garcia.

[58] U.S. Department of Homeland Security, U.S. Citizenship and Immigration Services, Consideration of Deferred Action for Childhood Arrivals Process, Frequently Asked Questions, http://www.uscis.gov/humanitarian/consideration-deferred-action-childhood-arrivals- process/frequently-asked-questions. For additional information on prosecutorial discretion and deferred action, see CRS Report R43782, *Executive Discretion as to Immigration: Legal Overview*, by Kate M. Manuel and Michael John Garcia, and CRS Report R42924, *Prosecutorial Discretion in Immigration Enforcement: Legal Issues*, by Kate M. Manuel and Todd Garvey.

[59] U.S. Department of Homeland Security, Memorandum to David V. Aguilar, Acting Commissioner, U.S. Customs and Border Protection, Alejandro Mayorkas, Director, U.S. Citizenship and Immigration Services, John Morton, Director, U.S. Immigration and Customs Enforcement, from Janet Napolitano, Secretary of Homeland Security, Exercising Prosecutorial Discretion with Respect to Individuals Who Came to the United States as Children, June 15, 2012.

[60] See CRS Report R43747, *Deferred Action for Childhood Arrivals (DACA): Frequently Asked Questions*, by Andorra Bruno.

[61] U.S. Department of Homeland Security, Memorandum to Leon Rodriguez, Director, U.S. Citizenship and Immigration Services, Thomas S. Winkowski, Acting Director, U.S. Immigration and Customs Enforcement, R. Gil Kerlikowske, Commissioner, U.S. Customs and Border Protection, from Jeh Charles Johnson, Secretary of Homeland Security, *Exercising Prosecutorial Discretion with Respect to Individuals Who Came to the United States as Children and with Respect to Certain Individuals Whose Parents are U.S. Citizens or Permanent Residents*, November 20, 2014.

[62] U.S. Department of Homeland Security, Memorandum to Leon Rodriguez, Director, U.S. Citizenship and Immigration Services, from Jeh Charles Johnson, Secretary of Homeland Security, *Families of U.S. Armed Forces Members and Enlistees*, November 20, 2014.

[63] INA §212(d)(5)(A).

[64] Individuals previously lawfully admitted to the United States, even if no longer in a lawful immigration status, are not considered eligible for parole. For this reason, as discussed above, the memorandum directs USCIS to consider the availability of deferred action for unauthorized family members of military service members and veterans who were previously lawfully admitted to the United States.

[65] See U.S. Department of Homeland Security, U.S. Citizenship and Immigration Services, *Parole of Spouses, Children and Parents of Active Duty Members of the U.S. Armed Forces, the Selected Reserve of the Ready Reserve, and Former Members of the U.S. Armed Forces or Selected Reserve of the Ready Reserve and the Effect of Parole on Inadmissibility under Immigration and Nationality Act § 2 l 2(a)(6)(A)(i)*, November 15, 2013.

[66] U.S. Department of Homeland Security, Memorandum to Leon Rodriguez, Director, U.S. Citizenship and Immigration Services, from Jeh Charles Johnson, Secretary of Homeland Security, *Families of U.S. Armed Forces Members and Enlistees*, November 20, 2014.

[67] The Board of Immigration Appeals in the Department of Justice is the highest administrative body for interpreting and applying immigration laws. BIA decisions are binding on all DHS officers and immigration judges unless modified or overruled by the Attorney General or a federal court.

[68] The INA enumerates grounds of inadmissibility—grounds upon which aliens are ineligible for visas and admission to the United States. For an overview of the INA grounds of inadmissibility, see CRS Report R43589, *Immigration: Visa Security Policies*, by Ruth Ellen Wasem, p. 5.

[69] U.S. Department of Homeland Security, Memorandum to Stevan E.Bunnell, General Counsel, Office of the General Counsel, Leon Rodriguez, Director, U.S. Citizenship and Immigration Services, Thomas S. Winkowski, Acting Director, U.S. Immigration and Customs Enforcement, R. Gil Kerlikowske, Commissioner, U.S. Customs and Border Protection, from Jeh Charles Johnson, Secretary of Homeland Security, *Directive to Provide Consistency Regarding Advance Parole*, November 20, 2014.

[70] See CRS Report R42866, *Permanent Legal Immigration to the United States: Policy Overview*, by William A. Kandel.

[71] There is no statutory restriction on submitting a visa petition on behalf of an alien who is in the United States without a lawful immigration status.

[72] INA §245(a).

[73] Spouses and minor children of U.S. citizens and parents of adult U.S. citizens, designated as "immediate relatives" under the family-based immigration system, do not have to wait for a visa number to become available. Other family-based immigrants are subject to a complex set of preference categories and numerical limits, and must wait for an immigrant visa number to be immediately available before they can apply for a visa..

[74] For example, there is an exception for the spouses and children of U.S. citizens and the parents of adult U.S. citizens (INA §245(c)). Another provision (INA §245(i)), which was last updated in 2000, enables aliens who entered the United States unlawfully to adjust status provided they meet other requirements. Among the requirements, the alien must be the beneficiary of a petition or application filed by April 30, 2001.

[75] U.S. Department of Homeland Security, Memorandum to Leon Rodriguez, Director, U.S. Citizenship and Immigration Services, from Jeh Charles Johson, Secretary of Homeland Security, *Expansion of the Provisional Waiver Program*, November 20, 2014.

[76] CRS Report R43745, *Temporary Professional, Managerial, and Skilled Foreign Workers: Legislation in the 113th Congress*, by Ruth Ellen Wasem.

[77] This section is adapted from archived CRS Report RL33977, *Immigration of Foreign Workers: Labor Market Tests and Protections*, by Ruth Ellen Wasem.

[78] Certain second preference immigrants whose admittance is deemed to be "in the national interest" are exempt from labor certification.

[79] This section is adapted from CRS Report R43735, *Temporary Professional, Managerial, and Skilled Foreign Workers: Policy and Trends*, by Ruth Ellen Wasem.

[80] Temporary visas are issued for an expressed purpose and a specific period of time. In most cases, the foreign national must demonstrate they have a "home they have no intention of abandoning" in their native country. For more background on temporary visas, see archived CRS Report RL31381, *U.S. Immigration Policy on Temporary Admissions*, by Ruth Ellen Wasem.

[81] U.S. Department of Homeland Security, Memorandum to Leon Rodriquez, Director, U.S. Citizenship and Immigration Services, and Thomas S. Winkowski, Acting Director, U.S. Immigration and Customs Enforcement, from Jeh Charles Johnson, Secretary of Homeland Security, *Policies Supporting U.S. High-Skilled Business and Workers*, November 20, 2014, p. 2.

[82] While the data include some unskilled and low-skilled workers as well as accompanying family members, visas for managerial, skilled, and professional workers dominate the trends. These data understate the trends in professional, managerial, and skilled foreign workers, because the State Department does not issue visas to nonimmigrants that change status within the United States. For example, a foreign national residing in the United States as a student may convert their status to a temporary nonimmigrant worker without going

abroad to obtain a new visa. Bureau of Consular Affairs, *Report of the Visa Office*, U.S. Department of State, Table XVI, multiple years.

[83] U.S. Department of Homeland Security, Memorandum to Leon Rodriquez, Director, U.S. Citizenship and Immigration Services, and Thomas S. Winkowski, Acting Director, U.S. Immigration and Customs Enforcement, from Jeh Charles Johnson, Secretary of Homeland Security, *Policies Supporting U.S. High-Skilled Business and Workers*, November 20, 2014 (hereafter, "the High-Skilled Memorandum").

[84] Previously, the Administration announced other policies with the goal of retaining high-skilled workers. For example, in May 2014, DHS published a proposed rule to grant work authorization to spouses of H-1B visa holders with approved petitions for LPR status. Department of Homeland Security, U.S. Citizenship and Immigration Services, "Employment Authorization for Certain H-4 Dependent Spouses," 79 *Federal Register* 26886-26901, May 12, 2014.

[85] Department of Labor, *Department of Labor to Pursue Modernized Recruitment and Application Requirements for the PERM Program*, Fact Sheet, Washington, DC, November 20, 2014.

[86] This section is adapted from CRS Report R42048, *Numerical Limits on Employment-Based Immigration: Analysis of the Per-Country Ceilings*, by Ruth Ellen Wasem.

[87] Ibid.

[88] Visa retrogression occurs when visa priority dates moved backward in time rather than forward in time. Most recently, in October 2014, a visa retrogression occurred in the second employment-based preference category for India. See Department of State, *Visa Bulletin, Immigrant Numbers for November 2014*, Washington, DC, October 9, 2014.

[89] INA §212(a)(5). *Labor certification* generally refers to the process in which employers must *document* in the application that certain conditions have been met, including that the employer has attempted to recruit of U.S. workers. As part of this process, the employer must also document the wages, working conditions, and benefits to be provided to foreign workers, thereby permitting DOL to certify that those conditions have been met. *Labor attestation* refers to a process in which employers *attest* that such conditions have been met but do not have to submit documentation with the application. Employers instead must retain documentation showing that the necessary conditions have been satisfied. For more information, see CRS Report R43223, *The Framework for Foreign Workers' Labor Protections Under Federal Law*, by Margaret Mikyung Lee and Jon O. Shimabukuro.

[90] The Program Electronic Review Management (PERM) regulations were published on December 27, 2004, after initially being proposed in May 2002. The stated goals of PERM are to streamline the labor certification process and reduce fraudulent filings. *Federal Register*, vol. 69, no. 247, Dec. 27, 2004, p. 77325.

[91] Department of Labor, *Department of Labor to Pursue Modernized Recruitment and Application Requirements for the PERM Program*, Fact Sheet, Washington, DC, November 20, 2014.

[92] Specifically DOL will seek input on: options for identifying labor force shortages and surpluses and methods for aligning domestic worker recruitment requirements with demonstrated shortages and surpluses; methods to modernize the U.S. worker recruitment requirement; processes to clarify employer obligations to insure PERM positions are fully open to U.S. workers; ranges of processing times and possibilities for premium processing; and the application submission and review process. *Ibid.*

[93] The High-Skilled Memorandum, p. 5.

[94] INA §203(b)(2)(B).

[95] Because no statutory or regulatory definition of "national interest" exists, USCIS relies on a 1998 Administrative Appeals Office precedent decision setting forth a three-prong test for evaluating requests for a national interest waiver. See Matter of New York State Department of Transportation, 22 I&N Dec. 215 (Comm'r 1998) ("NYSDOT"). U.S. Citizenship and Immigration Services, *National Interest Waiver*, Washington, DC.

[96] For an example of this argument, see Amar Toor, "Can Obama's immigration reform stop Silicon Valley's brain drain?," *The Verge*, January 30, 2013. Under the EB-5 category, the money invested by the foreign national must be legally owned by the investor. Matter of Ho, 22 I&N Dec. 206 (Assoc. Comm'r 1998).

[97] INA §212(d)(5).

[98] See CRS Report RL33809, *Noncitizen Eligibility for Federal Public Assistance: Policy Overview and Trends*, by Alison Siskin.

[99] See CRS Report R43561, *Treatment of Noncitizens Under the Affordable Care Act*, by Alison Siskin and Erika K. Lunder.

[100] For more on OPT, see archived CRS Report R42530, *Immigration of Foreign Nationals with Science, Technology, Engineering, and Mathematics (STEM) Degrees* , by Ruth Ellen Wasem.

[101] To qualify for the 17-month extension, F-1 students must have received STEM degrees included on the STEM Designated Degree Program List, be employed by employers enrolled in E-Verify, and have received an initial grant of post-completion OPT related to such a degree (i.e., already approved for 12 months in OPT). 8 C.F.R. 214.2(f)(10). E-Verify is an electronic employment eligibility verification program that U.S. employers voluntarily use to confirm the new hires' employment authorization through Social Security Administration and, if necessary, DHS databases. CRS Report R40446, *Electronic Employment Eligibility Verification*, by Andorra Bruno.

[102] This section is adapted from CRS Report R43745, *Temporary Professional, Managerial, and Skilled Foreign Workers: Legislation in the 113th Congress*, by Ruth Ellen Wasem.

[103] See CRS Report RL33977, *Immigration of Foreign Workers: Labor Market Tests and Protections*, by Ruth Ellen Wasem.

[104] For historical background, see archived CRS Report RL32030, *Immigration Policy for Intracompany Transfers (L Visa): Issues and Legislation*, by Ruth Ellen Wasem.

[105] Office of the Inspector General, *Review of Vulnerabilities and Potential Abuses of the L-1 Visa Program*, U.S. Department of Homeland Security, OIG-06-22, January 2006, p. 9.

[106] U.S. Department of Homeland Security, Memorandum to Leon Rodriquez, Director, U.S. Citizenship and Immigration Services, and Thomas S. Winkowski, Acting Director, U.S. Immigration and Customs Enforcement, from Jeh Charles Johnson, Secretary of Homeland Security, *Policies Supporting U.S. High-Skilled Business and Workers*, November 20, 2014, p. 4.

[107] The term immigrant is synonymous with lawful permanent resident (LPR), a person who has been legally admitted to the United States to reside permanently.

[108] Jeb Bush, Thomas F. McLarty III, and Edward Alden, *U.S. Immigration Policy*, Council on Foreign Relations, Independent Task Force Report No. 63, Washington, DC, 2009, p. 80 (hereafter *U.S. Immigration Policy*, 2009.)

[109] Examples include the Department of Education's Upward Bound Program, which facilitates college enrollment though academic preparation for first-generation college students from low-income families, and the Department of Labor Employment and Training Administration's National Farmworker Jobs Program, which helps seasonal farmworkers and their families attain greater economic stability.

[110] Attempts to create an office can be seen in H.R. 1617 introduced during the 112th Congress which sought to both rename USCIS's Office of Citizenship the Office of Citizenship and Immigrant Integration and to expand its mission accordingly.

[111] In 2006, President George W. Bush initiated the Task Force on New Americans as an inter-agency effort to help immigrants "learn English, embrace the common core of American civic culture, and fully become American." The Task Force worked to develop more cooperative federal approach to assimilation and included representatives from 20 federal agencies. See http://www.uscis.gov/archive/archive-news/fact-sheet-task-force-new-americans. In June 2010 the White House Domestic Policy Council formed the Interagency Working Group on the Federal Role of Immigrant Integration to assess the roles and

equities of the federal government in promoting immigrant integration and to better coordinate integration efforts across agencies. President Barack Obama's proposed 2010 budget included a $10 million allocation for a new Immigrant Integration Program in USCIS' Office of Citizenship that would have established a program devoted exclusively to helping legal immigrants transition into their new communities. See U.S. Government Accountability Office, *Immigrant Integration: U.S. Citizenship and Immigration Services Could Better Assess Its Grant Program*, GAO-12-274, Washington, DC, December 2011.

[112] The White House, Presidential Memorandum, *Creating Welcoming Communities and Fully Integrating Immigrants and Refugees*, November 21, 2014.

[113] S. 744 would have renamed USCIS's Office of Citizenship as the Office of Citizenship and New Americans (OCNA). OCNA's functions would have included promoting institutions and providing training and educational materials on aliens' citizenship responsibilities and providing general leadership, consultation, and coordination of such activities across federal agencies and with state and local entities. In coordination with the Task Force on New Americans (TFNA) established in 2006, OCNA would have: advised USCIS, DHS, and the Domestic Policy Council on challenges related to immigrant integration; established national integration goals; evaluated federal immigrant integration efforts; and identified and assessed integration implications of new and proposed immigration policies. In addition, OCNA would have coordinated with state and local governments on integration issues; coordinated with other federal agencies to do the same regarding education and English programs; assisted states with new immigrant integration grant programs; and required a report to Congress every two years. S. 744 §§2511, 2521-2524.

[114] The White House, Presidential Memorandum, *Creating Welcoming Communities and Fully Integrating Immigrants and Refugees*, November 21, 2014.

[115] See CRS Report R43366, *U.S. Naturalization Policy*, by William A. Kandel.

[116] The INA waives some of these requirements for applicants over age 50 with 20 years of U.S. residency, those with mental or physical disabilities, and those who have served in the U.S. military.

[117] See National Immigration Forum, Making the Naturalization Process Less Daunting by Reforming the USCIS Fee Structure, Washington, DC, 2011; commentary by the United States Conference of Catholic Bishops, Hebrew Immigrant Aid society, and Immigration Policy Center in National Foundation for American Policy, Reforming the Naturalization Process, NFAP Policy Brief, August 2011; and Joyce Baldwin, Helping Immigrants Become U.S. Citizens, Carnegie Corporation of New York, The New Americans Campaign, vol. 7, no. 2, Summer 2013 (hereafter "*Helping Immigrants*, 2013").

[118] Manuel Pastor, Jared Sanchez, and Rhonda Ortiz, et al., Nurturing Naturalization: Could Lowering the Fee Help?, Center for the Study of Immigrant Integration, University of Southern California, February 2013.

[119] See CRS Report R43366, *U.S. Naturalization Policy*, by William A. Kandel, pp. 15-18.

[120] See *Helping Immigrants* 2013 and commentary of the Catholic Conference of Bishops etc. NFAP Policy Brief 2011. Many also characterize the naturalization application forms and instructions as excessively complex and unclear, with potential legal consequences for incorrect responses. They contend that prospective naturalization petitioners may be deterred from applying, and that simplifying the language in the N-400 application and instructions would make the naturalization process more accessible. See commentary of Mary Giovagnoli, Immigration Policy Center, in National Foundation for American Policy, *Reforming the Naturalization Process*, NFAP Policy Brief, August 2011. Others raise concerns over the naturalization residency requirements which disadvantages LPRs based overseas for employment. Such individuals must wait until they physically reside in the United States to fulfill the naturalization requirements, prolonging their time required to naturalize. See commentary of Cyrus D. Mehta and Gary Endelman in National Foundation for American Policy, *Reforming the Naturalization Process*, NFAP Policy Brief, August 2011.

[121] U.S. Department of Homeland Security, Memorandum to Leon Rodriquez, Director, U.S. Citizenship and Immigration Services, from Jeh Charles Johnson, Secretary of Homeland Security, "*Policies to Promote and Increase Access to U.S. Citizenship*," November 20, 2014.

[122] U.S. Citizenship and Immigration Services is almost entirely funded through processing fees, a budgeting approach that contains inherent limitations on how much revenue can be raised to support USCIS operations. See CRS Report RL34040, *U.S. Citizenship and Immigration Services' Immigration Fees and Adjudication Costs: Proposed Adjustments and Historical Context*, by William A. Kandel.

[123] See for example *U.S. Immigration Policy*, 2009, pp. 90-95.

[124] Most recently, for example, S. 744, the Border Security, Economic Opportunity, and Immigration Modernization Act passed by the Senate in 2013, did not include explicit provisions to modernize the administrative functioning and infrastructure of USCIS.

[125] U.S. Department of Homeland Security, Office of Inspector General, *Major Management and Performance Challenges Facing the Department of Homeland Security*, OIG-15-09, November 14, 2014.

[126] The White House, Presidential Memorandum, "Modernizing and Streamlining the U.S. Immigrant Visa System for the 21st Century," November 21, 2014.

[127] Jeffrey S. Passel and D'Vera Cohn, *Unauthorized Immigrant Totals Rise in 7 States, Fall in 14: Decline in Those From Mexico Fuels Most State Decreases*, Pew Research Center, Washington, DC, November 18, 2014, p. 8. In 2012, the size of the civilian labor force was estimated at 157.7 million according to data from the 2012 American Community Survey. See "Factfinder" at Census.gov.

[128] For example, see Southern Policy Law Center, "Immigrant Justice," http://www.splcenter.org/what-we-do/immigrant-justice.

[129] Ibid.

[130] Unauthorized workers represents relatively large proportions of the workforce in particular industries, such as agriculture, construction, food handling, and low-skilled services. Jeffrey S Passel and D'Vera Cohn, *A Portrait of Unauthorized Immigrants in the United States*, Pew Research Center, Washington, DC, April 14, 2009.

[131] INA §274A. These cases also may involve additional violations, such as alien smuggling, document fraud, and worker exploitation. See. CRS Report R40002, *Immigration-Related Worksite Enforcement: Performance Measures*, by Andorra Bruno.

[132] U.S. Department of Homeland Security, USCIS fact sheet, *Worksite Enforcement Overview*, April 30, 2009.

[133] U.S. Department of Labor, *Revised Memorandum of Understanding between the Departments of Homeland Security and Labor Concerning Enforcement Activities at Worksites*, December 11, 2011.

[134] See for instance, National Immigration Law Center, "DHS Issues "New" Worksite Enforcement Guidelines That Are Simply More of the Same," press release, April 30, 2009.

[135] Thomas E. Perez, Secretary, U.S. Department of Labor, "Fact Sheet: Establishment of Interagency Working Group for the Consistent Enforcement of Federal Labor, Employment and Immigration Laws," November 21, 2014.

[136] For more on U and T statuses, see CRS Report RL34317, *Trafficking in Persons: U.S. Policy and Issues for Congress*, by Alison Siskin and Liana Rosen.

[137] Department of Homeland Security U.S. Citizenship and Immigration Services, Information for Law Enforcement Officials, *Immigration Relief for Victims of Human Trafficking and Other Crimes*, http://www.uscis.gov/sites/default/files/USCIS/ Resources/Humanitarian%20Based%20Benefits%20and%20Resources/TU_QAforLawEnforcement.pdf.

[138] Current policy allows DOL's Wage and Hour Division to certify trafficking victims for U status. While trafficking victims may be eligible for U status, only victims of severe forms of trafficking may qualify for T status. Department of Labor, *The Department of Labor's Wage and Hour Division Will Expand Its Support Of Victims of Human Trafficking and*

Other Crimes Seeking Immigration Relief from DHS, Fact Sheet, Washington, DC, November 20, 2014 ; and Department of Labor, "Secretary's Order 01-2014," vol. 79, no. 247 *Federal Register* 30224, December 24, 2014.

[139] Since 2011, DOL has provided law enforcement certification for U visa applications for the following crimes: trafficking, involuntary servitude, peonage, obstruction of justice, and witness tampering.

[140] For example, see Alliance to End Slavery and Trafficking, *DOL/Department of Wage and Hour, The Need for Funding and Report Language: $5,000,000 for services for victims of trafficking to implement Section 107(b) of the TVPA and report language*, http://endslaveryandtrafficking.org/fy2014/Department-of-Labor-Department-of-Wage-and-Hour.php.

INDEX

#

9/11, 78

A

abdication, vii, 1, 2, 3, 4, 18, 19, 28, 35, 41, 50, 51, 52, 65
abuse, 30
access, 100, 101
accountability, 34
accounting, 97
adaptation, 33, 64
adjudications, viii, 2
adjustment, 5, 9, 10, 16, 23, 31, 33, 46, 60, 92
Administrative Procedure Act, 25, 64, 65
adult literacy, 100
advancement, 89
adverse effects, 96
Afghanistan, 7
age, ix, 31, 40, 42, 88, 89, 115
agencies, viii, 8, 17, 25, 28, 39, 41, 42, 43, 47, 48, 52, 67, 74, 75, 79, 81, 85, 86, 100, 101, 103, 104, 105, 106, 109, 110, 114, 115
agency decisions, 64
agriculture, 116
Alaska, 37
alien smuggling, 31, 42, 116
APA, 25
appropriations, 35, 106
Appropriations Act, 66
armed conflict, 6, 29
arrest(s), 17, 43, 83, 86, 108
assessment, 99
assets, 79
assimilation, 101, 114
asylum, 4, 27, 30, 67, 108
Attorney General, 7, 12, 24, 27, 30, 33, 47, 48, 62, 63, 70, 82, 111
authority(s), vii, ix, 1, 2, 3, 4, 5, 7, 8, 9, 10, 12, 14, 15, 16, 26, 27, 30, 31, 33, 40, 41, 45, 47, 48, 49, 50, 51, 54, 58, 60, 63, 64, 66, 68, 75, 76, 82, 92, 93, 105

B

beneficiaries, 8, 22, 30, 37, 42, 44, 63, 89, 93
benefits, vii, 1, 2, 3, 5, 7, 14, 15, 16, 28, 33, 51, 53, 54, 55, 57, 63, 67, 68, 101, 103, 113
BIA, 10, 20, 24, 32, 33, 34, 36, 62, 63, 91, 111
blogs, 38, 70
Border Patrol, 78, 79, 80, 107, 108
border security, viii, x, 39, 40, 41, 73, 76, 77, 78, 79, 80, 81, 83, 106, 107, 109
brain, 114

brain drain, 114
businesses, 44, 98, 99, 103

C

CAP, 85, 110
Caribbean, 65
case law, 30
category a, 62
CBP, 74, 79, 80, 81, 85, 107, 108
Census, 116
certification, 24, 61, 74, 96, 97, 104, 105, 112, 113, 117
CFR, 68
challenges, ix, 40, 55, 57, 65, 69, 77, 78, 80, 81, 86, 103, 115
Chevron deference, 26, 28
childhood, 32, 60, 88, 111
children, vii, viii, 1, 12, 14, 22, 29, 31, 39, 40, 41, 42, 46, 48, 53, 54, 57, 63, 71, 74, 77, 79, 84, 88, 90, 92, 93, 94, 112
Chile, 7
China, 7
CIS, 35
citizens, viii, 12, 28, 31, 39, 40, 42, 44, 46, 48, 62, 65, 74, 89, 90, 91, 92, 93, 94, 101, 112
citizenship, 24, 53, 100, 101, 110, 115
classes, 12, 31, 93
classification, 45, 92, 97
Coast Guard, 74, 79, 81, 108
college students, 114
commerce, 36
commercial, 55, 80
common law, 33
common sense, 37
communication, 100
communities, 34, 47, 60, 110, 115
competition, 57, 70, 77
complexity, 103
conference, 3
consent, 66
Constitution, vii, ix, 1, 3, 4, 20, 33, 40, 41, 48, 50, 55, 57, 65, 68, 69
construction, 22, 28, 49, 116
controversial, x, 73, 76, 88
conviction, 10
cooperation, 85
coordination, 75, 80, 81, 102, 105, 106, 115
cosmetic(s), 36, 67
Court of Appeals, 24, 35, 56, 57, 60
Craftsmen, 70
crimes, 4, 17, 20, 31, 61, 75, 86, 105, 117
criminal activity, 9, 43, 51, 105, 106
criminal gangs, 17
criminals, 87
Cuba, 7, 12, 16
culture, 114
Customs and Border Protection, 74, 79, 108, 111, 112

D

DACA, vii, viii, 1, 3, 8, 17, 19, 20, 26, 27, 30, 32, 34, 35, 40, 41, 42, 52, 54, 56, 58, 59, 60, 63, 65, 67, 69, 71, 74, 78, 88, 89, 94, 106, 111
danger, 17, 84
database, 85, 110
defendants, 69
Deferred Action for Childhood Arrivals, vii, viii, 1, 3, 26, 32, 35, 39, 41, 42, 60, 68, 74, 78, 111
denial, 10, 46, 63
Department of Agriculture, 79
Department of Defense, 90
Department of Education, 100, 114
Department of Homeland Security, 6, 42, 64, 66, 74, 76, 107, 108, 109, 110, 111, 112, 113, 114, 116
Department of Justice, 63, 111
Department of Labor, 45, 61, 74, 76, 105, 113, 114, 116
Department of the Treasury, 68
Department of Transportation, 113
Deportations, 109
derivatives, 22, 23, 36, 37
detention, 66, 74, 82, 84, 86, 87, 108, 109
disability, 55
disclosure, 71

discretionary authority, vii, ix, 1, 2, 3, 4, 5, 7, 8, 33, 40, 41, 48, 50, 64, 92, 93
displacement, 99
disposition, 69
distribution, 109
District of Columbia, 35, 57
diversity, 95
DOJ, 24, 28, 30, 33, 64, 66, 85, 109, 110
DOL, 45, 46, 57, 59, 61, 62, 74, 75, 76, 95, 96, 97, 104, 105, 113, 116, 117
domestic labor, 12, 15, 70
Domestic Policy Council, 36, 114, 115
domestic violence, 63, 67, 109
Dominican Republic, 7
draft, 12, 23
Drug Enforcement Administration, 79
drug treatment, 35
drugs, 26, 67
dynamic systems, 107

E

Eastern Europe, 12
economic status, 36
education, 55, 95, 100, 115
educational materials, 115
El Salvador, 7, 29, 70
eligibility criteria, ix, 40, 42, 66, 74, 88
embassy, 92
emergency, 32
employees, 20, 23, 45, 56, 80, 95, 97, 99
employers, 44, 45, 46, 96, 97, 104, 113, 114
employment, ix, 3, 7, 8, 15, 20, 22, 23, 30, 32, 37, 40, 41, 42, 43, 44, 45, 47, 48, 56, 57, 58, 60, 61, 63, 69, 70, 74, 75, 77, 88, 89, 91, 94, 95, 96, 97, 98, 99, 104, 105, 113, 114, 115
employment authorization, ix, 7, 40, 41, 42, 43, 48, 57, 58, 74, 88, 89, 94, 114
employment opportunities, 45
enforcement priorities, x, 33, 51, 60, 66, 73, 76, 82, 83, 84, 85, 87, 106, 109
engineering, 44, 77
English Language, 100
enrollment, 114
entrepreneurs, 74
Environmental Protection Agency, 26
EPA, 26, 37
epidemic, 6
Equal Employment Opportunity Commission, 105
equipment, 107
equities, 115
espionage, 17, 83
Estonia, 12
Europe, 12
evidence, 16, 69, 102, 105
evolution, 109
exclusion, 9, 10, 12
execution, 19
executive branch, viii, 2, 3, 4, 5, 6, 7, 8, 12, 15, 16, 17, 18, 22, 23, 24, 33, 41, 48, 49, 50, 51, 52, 57, 63, 64, 100
Executive Order, 47
exercise, vii, ix, 1, 3, 4, 5, 8, 15, 16, 18, 22, 28, 31, 33, 34, 40, 41, 43, 49, 50, 58, 64, 65, 82, 83, 89
expenditures, 69
expertise, 36, 64
exploitation, 42, 104, 105, 109, 116

F

FAA, 37
Fair Labor Standards Act, 105
families, 93, 114
family members, 12, 28, 31, 32, 45, 53, 65, 74, 90, 91, 111, 112
family relationships, 95
FDA, 26
fear, 27, 29, 97
Federal Bureau of Investigation (FBI), 85, 110
Federal Communications Commission, 37
federal courts, 8, 20, 25, 55
federal criminal law, 50
Federal Emergency Management Agency, 108
federal government, 56, 115

federal law, viii, 2, 8, 15, 48, 50, 53, 60, 64, 79
Federal Register, 29, 113, 117
fencing, 79, 107
financial, 10, 31, 69
fingerprints, 85, 110
Finland, 12
flexibility, 4, 33, 64, 74
food, 36, 55, 67, 68, 116
force, 36, 47, 61, 64, 75, 97, 101, 102, 105, 114
foreign nationals, vii, 2, 3, 44, 82, 86, 94, 96, 97, 98, 100, 105
foreign-born population, 100
fraud, 9, 10, 31, 46, 65, 103, 105, 116
freedom, 28
funding, 66, 75, 77, 102, 104, 105
funds, 35, 55

G

GAO, 115
global competition, 96
governor, 69
grand jury, 64
grant programs, 115
grants, vii, 2, 3, 4, 5, 7, 12, 17, 18, 20, 35, 42, 43, 51, 52, 58, 101
growth, 79, 100
Guantanamo, 12
Guatemala, 29
guidance, 5, 17, 24, 52, 57, 60, 71, 75, 82, 91, 97, 98, 100, 104, 109
guidelines, 18, 30, 35, 36, 60, 63, 64

H

Harvard Law School, 37
health, 10, 54, 55, 68, 100
health care, 54, 68
health care programs, 54
health insurance, 68
higher education, 44, 55
hiring, 7, 15, 104
history, 12, 66, 101
Honduras, 29
Hong Kong, 12
House, 61, 77, 98, 107, 108
housing, 55
human, 46, 75, 106
Hungary, 7, 12

I

identification, 50, 66, 86
illegal aliens, 69
immigrants, 11, 22, 23, 31, 34, 37, 45, 47, 59, 69, 70, 76, 95, 96, 97, 100, 101, 102, 112, 114
Immigration Accountability Executive Action, v, ix, 73, 76, 78, 106
Immigration Act, 26, 65, 66, 71
Immigration and Customs Enforcement (ICE), 20, 28, 33, 34, 35, 56, 60, 61, 62, 69, 71, 74, 79, 81, 82, 84, 85, 86, 87, 99, 104, 108, 109, 110, 111, 112, 113, 114
Immigration and Nationality Act, vii, ix, 1, 3, 32, 40, 41, 70, 77, 82, 88, 111
immigration matters, vii, 1, 2, 3
immunity, 50
Impact Assessment, 110
imprisonment, 10, 36
inadmissible, 9, 10, 11, 12, 27, 31, 88, 91, 92
income, 98, 100, 102, 114
increased competition, 57
India, 113
individuals, 16, 19, 23, 34, 68, 77, 86, 88, 89, 91, 94, 100, 115
industry(s), 37, 57, 104, 116
information sharing, 17, 43, 81, 85
information technology, 99
infrastructure, 79, 103, 107, 116
injury, 20, 55, 56, 69
INS, 12, 16, 28, 30, 32, 33, 34, 37, 47, 61, 62, 63, 67, 70, 82, 110
institutions, 44, 55, 99, 115
integration, x, 73, 75, 76, 78, 80, 81, 100, 101, 102, 115

integrity, 74, 109
interoperability, 85
inventors, 45, 48, 96
investment(s), 98, 102
investors, 95, 98
Iran, 7
issues, vii, viii, 2, 22, 24, 48, 59, 68, 71, 77, 82, 87, 100, 101, 115
iteration, 79

J

job creation, 98
jurisdiction, ix, 16, 20, 24, 40, 52, 55, 56, 109
juveniles, 95

L

labor force, 113, 116
labor market, 99
Latin America, 12
Latinos, 109
Latvia, 12
law enforcement, 42, 61, 79, 83, 85, 86, 87, 100, 105, 107, 110, 117
laws, vii, 1, 3, 8, 18, 19, 27, 41, 59, 65, 68, 69, 75, 77, 104, 105, 111
leadership, 82, 115
Lebanon, 7
legal issues, 48, 49, 111
legislation, ix, 7, 12, 22, 23, 40, 54, 58, 75, 76, 77, 86, 88
legislative authority, 68
Liberia, 47
litigation, ix, 40, 60, 70
living conditions, 29
local government, 115
Louisiana, 69
LPRs, ix, 10, 12, 28, 31, 32, 40, 42, 44, 46, 47, 48, 53, 65, 67, 74, 75, 87, 89, 90, 91, 93, 94, 96, 101, 115

M

magnitude, 37
majority, 24, 97
management, 86
marriage, 34
Maryland, 68
mathematics, 44, 77
matter, 22, 27, 28, 30, 46, 48, 49, 50, 54, 63
media, 62
Medicaid, 54, 68
medical, 12, 68, 69
medical care, 68
Medicare, 68
membership, 27, 28, 29
mental illness, 84
Mexico, 29, 79, 116
migration, 6, 29, 42, 78, 79
military, 65, 69, 74, 90, 94, 111, 115
minimum wage, 104
mission(s), 80, 81, 82, 104, 114
modernization, 103
morale, 86
MPI, 26, 106
multinational firms, 99
murder, 31

N

narcotics, 79
national policy, 100
national security, 10, 17, 83, 84, 85, 86, 87, 109
nationality, 27, 28, 29, 110
natural disaster(s), 29
naturalization, x, 33, 46, 62, 73, 76, 78, 101, 102, 106, 115
Nicaragua, 7
nonenforcement, viii, 2, 4, 7, 19, 35
nonprofit organizations, 101

O

Obama, v, 3, 7, 8, 17, 20, 26, 27, 34, 38, 39, 41, 44, 45, 46, 48, 49, 50, 52, 55, 57, 58, 59, 61, 62, 69, 70, 79, 88, 109, 110, 111, 114, 115
Obama Administration, v, 3, 7, 8, 17, 20, 27, 34, 38, 39, 41, 44, 45, 46, 48, 49, 50, 52, 55, 57, 58, 59, 79, 88, 111
obstruction, 117
offenders, 17, 19
Office of the Inspector General, 103, 114
officials, viii, 2, 3, 4, 5, 7, 9, 10, 11, 12, 17, 24, 27, 28, 30, 31, 33, 47, 58, 59, 61, 64, 65, 101
on-the-job training, 75
operations, 45, 80, 116
opportunities, 75
outsourcing, 99

P

parents, 12, 18, 29, 46, 53, 57, 63, 65, 74, 89, 90, 94, 112
parole, viii, 2, 11, 12, 32, 43, 44, 45, 58, 60, 61, 63, 65, 70, 74, 78, 83, 88, 90, 91, 94, 98, 106, 111
penalties, 3
PEP, 43, 74, 86, 87
permission, 3, 16, 51
permit, viii, 2, 5, 7, 11, 12, 16, 23, 30, 31, 45, 48
POEs, 79, 108
Poland, 7, 12
policy, vii, x, 2, 4, 6, 17, 18, 19, 20, 24, 26, 28, 33, 35, 36, 37, 44, 50, 51, 56, 62, 63, 64, 65, 69, 73, 76, 78, 82, 83, 84, 85, 86, 87, 90, 94, 96, 97, 99, 100, 102, 106, 108, 109, 116
policy choice, 62
policy makers, 96
politics, 26, 70
population, viii, 19, 34, 35, 39, 41, 42, 43, 51, 58, 66, 74, 77, 87, 88, 93, 100
poverty, 30, 60, 63, 102
precedent(s), ix, 33, 40, 57, 63, 113
president, v, vii, viii, ix, 1, 3, 7, 19, 26, 27, 32, 36, 38, 39, 40, 41, 47, 50, 59, 61, 62, 65, 69, 73, 74, 75, 76, 78, 84, 85, 86, 87, 93, 97, 101, 102, 103, 104, 105, 106, 108, 114
President Clinton, 7, 47
President Obama, vii, viii, ix, 1, 39, 41, 65, 69, 73, 76
principles, 28, 60
prisoners, 12, 36
prisons, 110
professionals, 95
project, 80
proposition, 68
protection, 15, 37, 78, 94
public interest, 12, 32, 48, 84, 98
public safety, 17, 51, 83, 84, 109
publishing, 96
Puerto Rico, 79, 107

R

race, 27, 28, 29
recognition, 43, 64
recommendations, 75, 101, 103
redundancy, 103
reform(s), 16, 19, 26, 37, 46, 70, 71, 77, 79, 82, 86, 87, 101, 103, 107, 108, 110, 111, 114
refugees, 12, 29, 32, 58, 67
regulations, viii, 2, 8, 12, 24, 25, 26, 30, 31, 48, 60, 63, 70, 74, 75, 86, 93, 96, 97, 98, 99, 100, 113
reimburse, 69
relatives, 12, 22, 37, 44, 46, 58, 62, 93, 101, 112
relief, vii, viii, 1, 2, 3, 5, 6, 7, 8, 10, 14, 15, 18, 19, 20, 27, 28, 30, 32, 35, 39, 40, 41, 42, 47, 50, 51, 53, 55, 58, 60, 66, 68, 71, 88, 93, 109
religion, 27, 28, 29

requirements, vii, ix, 1, 2, 4, 8, 10, 20, 24, 28, 31, 32, 37, 40, 41, 45, 55, 57, 68, 69, 91, 92, 94, 98, 101, 104, 112, 113, 115
researchers, 45, 48, 95, 96, 98
resistance, 34
resources, 16, 19, 26, 33, 42, 51, 59, 66, 76, 79, 83, 84, 87, 104, 106, 107, 108
response, 7, 75, 76, 80, 107, 110
responsiveness, 74
restitution, 69
restrictions, 3, 5, 14, 15, 54, 70
retirement, 55
revenue, 102, 106, 116
rights, 104
risk(s), 17, 42, 68, 84, 85, 86, 109
Romania, 7
rules, 3, 24, 25, 36, 63, 75
rural areas, 95

S

safety, 10
sanctions, vii, 1, 50
science, 44, 77
scope, vii, 1, 3, 28, 43, 50, 51, 65, 75, 76, 88, 109
Secretary of Homeland Security, viii, 7, 12, 24, 27, 30, 34, 35, 39, 42, 47, 48, 108, 109, 110, 111, 112, 113, 114, 116
security, ix, 10, 77, 79, 80, 81, 84, 101, 107
Senate, 12, 77, 88, 98, 101, 107, 111, 116
sensors, 81, 107
September 11, 78
services, 46, 55, 57, 102, 103, 116, 117
sexual abuse, 109
short supply, 95
shortfall, 102
Silicon Valley, 114
skilled workers, x, 73, 76, 95, 100, 112, 113
social group, 27, 28, 29
Social Security, 114
Social Security Administration, 114
society, 100, 102, 115
Somalia, 29
Southwest border, x, 73, 76, 79
Soviet Union, 12
speech, 41
stability, 44, 114
staffing, 79
stakeholders, 101, 103
state(s), 6, 8, 19, 22, 29, 43, 52, 53, 54, 56, 57, 60, 66, 67, 68, 69, 75, 79, 80, 83, 84, 85, 86, 87, 97, 100, 101, 104, 108, 109, 110, 115
statistics, 84
statutes, viii, 2, 4, 5, 19, 20, 22, 27, 48, 49, 51, 58, 59, 65, 67
statutory authority, viii, 2, 12, 48, 58, 64, 66
structure, 33, 74, 80, 86, 103
subgroups, 93
substance abuse, 35
Supreme Court, viii, 2, 18, 20, 22, 25, 26, 49, 56
surveillance, 17, 79, 107
Sweden, 12

T

tariff, 37
Task Force, 81, 82, 101, 108, 114, 115
tax credits, 98
tax system, 103
taxpayers, 102
technical assistance, 101
technology(s), 44, 61, 77, 98, 103, 107
tensions, 95, 96
terrorism, 17, 83
terrorist attack, 78
terrorists, 79
threats, 79, 83
trafficking, 46, 75, 105, 106, 109, 116, 117
training, 44, 95, 96, 101, 115
treatment, 12, 35, 86
TVPA, 117

U

U.S. citizens, viii, 3, 12, 18, 22, 28, 31, 37, 39, 40, 42, 44, 46, 48, 53, 62, 65, 74, 89, 90, 91, 92, 93, 94, 101, 112
U.S. Department of Labor, 95, 116
U.S. immigration law, 79, 103, 110
U.S. immigration policies, ix, 73, 76
U.S. immigration system, x, 73, 76, 93, 103
U.S. labor market, 45, 95
unauthorized aliens, x, 7, 19, 73, 76, 77, 79, 87, 88, 89, 90, 92, 104, 106
uniform, 43, 96
uninsured, 68
USA, 61, 107

V

vessels, 107
victims, 34, 46, 61, 75, 78, 105, 106, 116, 117
Vietnam, 7
violent criminals, 17
visa system, 46, 61, 78, 95
vote, 101

W

wages, 45, 57, 95, 104, 105, 113
waiver, 8, 9, 10, 11, 27, 28, 31, 46, 74, 83, 92, 93, 98, 102, 113
Washington, 68, 80, 106, 107, 109, 110, 113, 114, 115, 116, 117
weapons, 79
weapons of mass destruction, 79
welfare, 10, 55
White House, 26, 41, 70, 74, 76, 101, 102, 103, 107, 114, 115, 116
workers, 12, 32, 44, 45, 57, 70, 74, 75, 77, 78, 91, 95, 96, 97, 98, 99, 104, 105, 112, 113, 116
workforce, 74, 86, 100, 104, 116
working conditions, 45, 57, 95, 97, 104, 113
workplace, 46, 106

Y

yield, 100, 102